D0824572

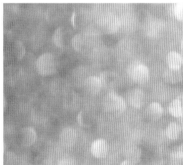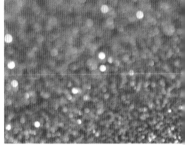

PERFECT PAMPERING FOR YOUR POOCH

Diva Dogs

LOUISE HARRIS

**SIMON &
SCHUSTER**
Illustrated

London · New York · Sydney · Toronto · New Delhi

A CBS COMPANY

First published in Great Britain
by Simon & Schuster UK Ltd, 2012
A CBS COMPANY

Copyright © Louise Harris, 2012

www.divadogs.co.uk

10 9 8 7 6 5 4 3 2 1

SIMON & SCHUSTER ILLUSTRATED BOOKS
Simon & Schuster UK Ltd
222 Gray's Inn Road
London
WC1X 8HB

www.simonandschuster.co.uk

Simon & Schuster Australia, Sydney
Simon & Schuster India, New Delhi

A CIP catalogue record for this book is available from
the British Library

ISBN 978-1-47110-154-0

Editorial director: Francine Lawrence
Design: XAB Design
Photography: Ruth Jenkinson
Production manager: Katherine Thornton
Commercial director: Ami Richards

Printed and bound in China
Colour reproduction by Dot Gradations Ltd, UK

Additional photographs:
Notebook image on pp.19-45: Creative Crop, Digital Vision,
Getty Images; Bubbles on pp.104–5: Photographer's Choice,
artpartner-images, Getty Images; Boots on p.118 courtesy of
the author

Note: All the dogs featured in this book are natural-born divas.
They are much-loved family members pampered for their
enjoyment and well-being.
The information contained in *Diva Dogs* is not intended as a
substitute for consulting your vet, with whom all matters relating
to your dog's health and welfare should always be discussed.

CONTENTS

ONCE UPON
A TIME

1

Sometimes it's the smallest things that make the biggest difference. In my case, that small thing was Lola, a tiny bundle of love who changed my life.

A STAR IS **BORN**

I wasn't always a doggy person. We didn't have dogs in my family and I never really saw dogs as best friends.

Growing up in the East End of London, the dogs around me tended to be tough ones that often seemed more frightening than friendly.

Before Lola turned my life around, I was working in London as a high-flying City analyst. I was doing 12-hour days and the work was stressful and demanding. I often went straight from the office to some work do or social drinks thing. Stocks went up, shares went down, and I went to parties and bought a lot of clothes. It was work hard, play hard. Fashion, fun, finance – that was my life. My world revolved around work colleagues – there was certainly no room in my life for a dog.

I had no idea that my destiny was about to be taken walkies down an entirely different path. After all, nobody expects their world to be turned upside down by a Yorkshire terrier.

It wasn't my idea to get a dog. My little sister Olivia got it into her head that she wanted a puppy and started obsessing about some dog she'd found on the internet. She nagged and nagged until, eventually, me and Mum had had enough. We agreed to investigate visiting a breeder – just to look, we said. Famous last words… Then, along came Lola.

Right from the beginning it was obvious that Lola wasn't just a pet, she was a personality. When she first arrived she was so small I could hold her in the palm of my hand. She was like a really teeny, tiny teddy bear – just so cute. But what she lacked in size she made up for in star quality. I just knew she was a diva and deserved the very best.

I was ready for a career change but I'd been putting off making any big decisions. Lola gave me the push I needed to turn my back on my City career and jump straight into the doggy fashion world. A lot of people thought I was mad, but in return Lola has taught me valuable lessons about love and responsibility and I've never looked back.

My dogs are part of my family. I now have four adorable furbabies – Lola, Lulu, Lolly and Larry – and I love spoiling them. Nothing is more important than making them feel special. Lola's love of luxury and pampering inspired me to open my own pet boutique and grooming parlour, and this is how Diva Dogs was born. My dream was to create a pooch paradise, a place where our furry friends would feel fabulous. We all want our dogs to be happy and healthy and a little pampering goes a long way to help a dog feel the love.

Since starting Diva Dogs I've met so many other people who love their doggies as much as I love mine. It's been lovely getting to know so many wonderful canine characters and their human mums and dads. One of the best things about Diva Dogs is that I get to build up a personal connection with our regular clientele. Our doggy customers are funny, quirky, cute and absolutely adorable. Each one of these gorgeous dogs is unique, with their own personality and needs. Not all dogs are party animals, but some pooches are natural-born show-offs who just love to be the centre of attention. Then there are the clowns of the canine world who live to entertain. Whatever your dog's personality, there's one thing every dog has to give – unconditional love.

Having dogs in my life has been such an amazing experience. I want to share everything I've learnt and I hope I will inspire you to give your pooch the star treatment and have fun together. With the help of Lola and her furry friends, I've got masses of tips on how to spoil your dog rotten.

This book will guide you through day-to-day doggy care, from what to feed your pooch and where they should sleep to keeping them fit and healthy. There are sections on travelling in style, communicating with your dog, how to make the most of playtime and helping your dog make friends with other pets and people. The book also introduces a few of Lola's friends and looks at some of my favourite breeds, with advice on getting the right pampering regime for your dog's breed and individual temperament.

Of course, the diva dog loves glamour so there's plenty of advice on high-quality pampering, dressing to impress and how to cope with a bad hair day. More than anything else, I hope that spending time indulging your dog will bring you closer together so you can both enjoy a happy, loving and very special friendship.

IS YOUR POOCH A DIVA DOG?

Most dogs have a touch of the diva in them. Look at me, play with me, cuddle me, stop what you're doing and be with me – now! They love attention, they adore being stars. Never try to upstage a diva dog. No matter how good you look, your diva dog is cuter and definitely has more appealing eyes.

Diva dogs often come in small packages. Pugs, Chihuahuas, shih-tzus and, of course, Yorkies are all famous for their glamour and flair. Most of these tiny dogs have been carefully bred over many generations specially to be companions – which is why they're so good at it. But dogs don't necessarily have to be small to have pizzazz. Whatever their size, diva dogs are always stylish and they simply don't do dull and dowdy. They appreciate luxuries and they expect that extra-special treatment. No hard floors for them, they want a fabulously soft bed to sleep on. They might get a bit mud-splashed on a walk, but they don't stay that way for long.

Like any star, the diva dog values good grooming and salon glamour. Scruffiness is not an option – it's all about sleek, silky shine and picture-perfect presentation. These precious pooches are health-conscious, too. They stick to a sensible exercise regime and watch what they eat.

The true diva dog is, naturally, loved to pieces and nothing you can do is too good for them. Treat your diva dog right, and you've guaranteed yourself a lifetime of love and loyalty.

LOLA'S
FRIENDS

Big or small, smooth or curly – all dogs are our best friends. But with so many adorable pooches to choose from, how do you know which one is the ideal companion for you?

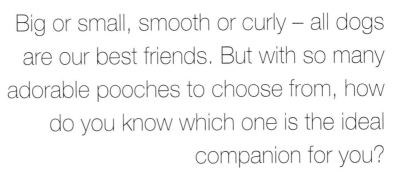

WHAT BREED
IS RIGHT FOR ME?

There are more than 200 breeds of pedigree dog, all with their own particular traits and quirks. They come in all shapes and sizes and have different grooming and exercise needs.

Of course, every pooch is an individual, but learning a bit about the characteristics of different breeds will help you make sure you're getting the dog that's right for you.

Be honest with yourself about what you have to offer. Are you happy to vacuum frequently if you get a dog that moults? Do you want a dog that doesn't need trips to the grooming parlour? Will you really enjoy brushing your dog every day or will it soon become a chore? Bichons and poodles, for example, need lots of brushing. If you don't fancy that, you might be better with a smooth-coated breed such as a pug or dachshund.

Bear in mind that all pups start off small, so look into how big they'll be when they're fully grown. Speak to as many people as possible who know about the breed you're interested in. Any responsible breeder will be happy to answer your questions and let you meet their dogs. In short, use

some common sense and get a dog that will be truly happy to share your life.

People often have very strong opinions about the type of dog they'd like to have in their lives. Some people are drawn to a breed they've had before or a dog they find particularly attractive. Some of us want a dog like one we've seen in a film or with our favourite celebrity.

Whatever type you choose, remember your pooch has to be right for the lifestyle you're living now. We all like to be on-trend, but don't be a fashion fad follower when it comes to choosing your best friend. It's important to ask yourself if you're the right person for your dog.

With so many different kinds of dog to choose from, it can be hard to know where to begin. So let me introduce you to some of Lola's lovely friends to help get you started.

CARE GUIDE KEY FOR PAGES 19–45

 weekly quick brush and go

needs coat care several times a week

 high maintenance, daily pampering

"My friend Yoda the French bulldog is a cuddly, happy, chubby little soul. Plus-size doggies are cute too!"

CHARACTER TRAITS

The Frenchie is a delightful character who looks like a little toughie but is actually very affectionate and friendly. French bulldogs can be strong-willed and will pull on the lead if they're not properly trained, but they are lots of fun and easy to train. They love to be at the centre of family life and will get on with well-mannered children, although they can be a bit cautious with strangers.

CARE GUIDE

The Frenchie's coat is easy to care for and just needs regular brushing to remove loose hair. The folds of skin on the face need to be washed frequently and their eyes should be kept clean. They don't need much exercise but do enjoy daily walks and lots of fun and games. Because of their short noses, they can easily become overheated in hot weather and need to be kept cool.

DID YOU KNOW?

The French bulldog is descended from toy bulldogs, which were taken to France by English lace makers looking for work.

LOOKS FABULOUS IN...

Frenchies are similar to bulldogs and pugs, so parka-style coats and hooded tops are a great look. Materials that stretch are always a good choice as these dogs have deep chests and their clothes should fit comfortably.

Yoda

FRENCH BULLDOG

Chic? Moi?
Must be my
Parisian roots
showing

CHECK LIST

SIZE Medium-small, but compact and heavy

COLOUR Most common colours include brindle, fawn and pied (two colours)

COAT TYPE short and smooth

CARE GUIDE

CHARACTER TRAITS

Yorkies are bold, lively little dogs who love to be boss. They might be tiny, but they still have the typical terrier traits of courage and confidence and they love to chase things and play games. They enjoy being involved in whatever you're doing and can be very attention-seeking. They demand respect and will not tolerate rough play from small children. Yorkies tend to dominate, if you let them, and can be quick to bark at anything and everything.

CARE GUIDE

Yorkies are full of energy and need daily walks and frequent play sessions. Show Yorkies have full, flowing coats, which look wonderful but take an awful lot of work to maintain. Most pet Yorkies have their hair cut, which should be done by a professional groomer. Even if your Yorkie has a trim, they will still need daily brushing. If left long, their fringes should be kept out of their eyes with a cute top knot.

DID YOU KNOW?

Yorkshire terriers were originally bred to hunt mice and rats in Yorkshire coal mines and textile mills.

LOOKS FABULOUS IN...

Yorkies are often seen wearing pretty red bows. Red is a colour that really suits them so, although we girls love pink, I generally suggest red as the best colour for Yorkies. If you have a Yorkie in full coat, it's a shame to hide their wonderful, flowing tresses, so don't overdo the dressing-up. Pretty collars and hair accessories are enough. Yorkies that are trimmed can wear just about anything. As they are so small, it's easy to find cute outfits for them so invest in something flamboyant to showcase your little diva.

"Minnie is a Yorkshire terrier like me. She is a perfect poser with a catwalk strut – she just loves the camera."

Minnie

YORKSHIRE TERRIER

Do I look cute in this? Of course I do!

CHECK LIST

SIZE — Tiny – small enough to fit in the palms of your hands

COLOUR — steel blue and tan

COAT TYPE Long and silky

CARE GUIDE

"Like all pugs my pal Billy is caring and loyal. He's also very handsome and never fails to make me laugh and smile."

CHARACTER TRAITS

Pugs make perfect companions and love nothing more than to be with their human parents. They are adaptable, affectionate and good-natured and love to make everyone laugh. Pugs don't tend to be barkers, but they can be stubborn and are experts at training humans to cater for their every whim.

CARE GUIDE

Pugs don't need lots of exercise, but they will enjoy short walks or play sessions. They tend to wheeze and snore and may be uncomfortable in hot weather. Their eyes are sensitive to dust and should be cleaned regularly, as should the wrinkles around their nose. The pug's coat is easy to look after. They do shed quite a lot, but brushing a couple of times a week will remove dead hair. Pugs are prone to putting on weight, so it's important not to overfeed them.

DID YOU KNOW?

Pugs originally came from China and were brought to Europe by sailors in the 1400s.

LOOKS FABULOUS IN...

Pugs are stout little characters and the boys look very good in butch outfits. Camo print and faux leather are a great mix. Little girl pugs are picture-perfect in most colours and pretty hoodies look absolutely divine.

Billy
PUG

i'm not frowning – i'm just thinking hard...

CHECK LIST

SIZE *small, but surprisingly heavy*

COLOUR *silver, apricot, fawn or black*

COAT TYPE *smooth, soft and short*

CARE GUIDE

CHARACTER TRAITS

Chihuahuas are intelligent, alert, confident little dogs with bags of character. These adorable dogs make wonderful companions and are extremely loyal to their owners. They can be suspicious of strangers and are not always keen on small children. Chihuahuas can get on with other dogs, but they particularly enjoy the company of their own kind. A natural watchdog, they can be quite noisy.

CARE GUIDE

Chihuahuas are ideal for city life and will happily live in a flat, so long as they have short, daily walks and lots of playtime. They are intelligent dogs and may get into mischief if they are not properly trained. Both coat types are easy to maintain. They do shed, but weekly grooming will remove dead hair.

DID YOU KNOW?

The Chihuahua is named after a region of Mexico, which is thought to be the breed's ancestral home.

LOOKS FABULOUS IN…

Smooth-coated Chi's are easy to dress and there are tons of wonderful items to choose from for dogs this size. Diamante collars and necklaces are just perfect on long-haired Chi's. Light fawn and cream-coloured Chi's look particularly amazing in pink. Male Chi's look great in baby blue, or a subtle camo may be just the thing for our more butch boys. Nail painting is great for smooth-coated Chi's – you can co-ordinate a splash of paw colour with your favourite fashion piece.

"My friend Chloe the Chihuahua loves being dressed up and she has that total diva look going on."

Chloe

CHIHUAHUA

Good things really do come in small packages

CHECK LIST

SIZE — Tiny – officially the smallest breed of dog in the world

COLOUR — Many colours, most common are tan, fawn, cream, white and black

COAT TYPE — Two coat types: smooth and glossy or long and wavy

CARE GUIDE

"Bow the poodle is such a classy girl. She looks great with a pretty bow in her beautiful jet black hair."

CHARACTER TRAITS

The poodle is extremely intelligent as well as good-looking and loves to be the entertainer. These lively, happy dogs are devoted to their owners and ever eager to please. They expect a lot of attention from their friends, but they are quick to return the favour. They respond really well to training and love to do tricks or take part in activities such as agility or obedience.

CARE GUIDE

The poodle's coat doesn't shed, but all that hair does need a lot of work. All poodles need brushing and combing several times a week as well as one or two baths a month. It's also recommended that they visit a professional groomer several times a year. Poodles are still working dogs at heart and they have a lot of energy. All three sizes are athletic and enjoy exercise. The standard, in particular, needs a good walk of at least an hour a day.

DID YOU KNOW?

Poodles were originally used to hunt ducks, and they are still expert swimmers to this day.

LOOKS FABULOUS IN…

Poodles are natural diva dogs and ooze sophistication and class. Most poodle haircuts are elaborate enough to keep them ahead of the fashion trend. However, as many of them enjoy parading their elegance, pretty hair bows always look good and are especially cute on both ears, as if they have bunches. A poodle will always look good in high-quality items such as pearls and luxurious materials like faux suede and faux fur.

Bow
POODLE

Who says you can't have brains as well as looks?

CHECK LIST

SIZE — Mini, small and large — a size to suit everyone

COLOUR — Many colours — most common include white, apricot, cream, brown, black and blue

COAT TYPE — short, dense, woolly curls

CARE GUIDE

"Blue the miniature dachshund is a clever little dog who goes to work with his human partner. He loves sitting on laps at meetings!"

CHARACTER TRAITS

Affectionately known as sausage dogs, miniature dachshunds are lively, fun-loving characters with a cheerful outlook. They have no idea how small they are and are very plucky, confident little dogs, forever getting into mischief. They form strong bonds with their owners, but can become bossy if not checked and may be a bit wary of strangers.

CARE GUIDE

Long- and wire-haired dachshunds need a good brushing at least once a week. Wire-haired dachsies also need to have their coats stripped two or three times a year, preferably by a professional groomer. The smooth-haired dachshund is easier to maintain simply with regular brushing to remove loose and dead hair. Despite their tiny legs, miniature dachshunds need at least one good walk a day and they love to hunt and dig. They are fond of food and will quickly become overweight if their diet is not controlled.

DID YOU KNOW?

Dachshund means 'badger dog' and they are named after the animals they were traditionally used to hunt.

LOOKS FABULOUS IN…

Dachsies are sometimes hard to dress because of their teeny legs, but they can be just as diva-ish as any other breed. Opt for fabrics like cotton and simple designs – they can look overdressed in highly patterned outfits. Little black and tan dachsies look really good in tan-coloured outfits, which complement their markings. I wouldn't dress them in black as this can get totally lost and look very dull.

Blue
MINIATURE DACHSHUND

Yes, I do like sausages!

CHECK LIST

SIZE — Tiny – short little legs with a very long back

COLOUR — Many colours – most common include black, red, golden, brown, grey, dapple or black and tan

COAT TYPE — Long; smooth; or wire-haired

CARE GUIDE

"My friend Roley the Pomeranian is just the cutest. He's cheeky and full of fun, and loves playing with his furry friends and cuddling up with his human parents."

CHARACTER TRAITS

The foxy-faced Pomeranian is a true extrovert. Dainty as a ballet dancer, this gorgeous ball of fluff is sweet-natured and makes a loving companion. They are cheeky little characters who are eager for attention and love to entertain. Pomeranians are very affectionate to their owners but can be wary of strangers.

CARE GUIDE

Pomeranians will happily live in a city, but they do enjoy a good walk. They are easy to train and love to learn tricks. The Pom's gorgeous coat should not really be cut as this will change the texture of your fluffy one, but you may trim around the ears and feet. Poms need a thorough brush several times a week to maintain coat quality and condition. The eyes should be kept clean to prevent staining. A professional groom several times a year will help keep a Pom's coat looking beautiful.

DID YOU KNOW?

The little Pom is related to much larger sled-dogs from the Arctic region.

LOOKS FABULOUS IN…

Poms are most commonly ruby or fawn and they look absolutely amazing in green, which really brings out the vibrant shades in their coats. Poms can wear clothes but remember that because they have so much fur they may need a size bigger – you don't want them to look like a tightly packed sausage. Don't make the mistake of buying a collar that is so wide you can see it through their fur. They have delicate little necks and don't need a neck brace. Make your Pom look pretty with lovely hair accessories or a patterned jacket or dress-style harness.

Roley

POMERANIAN

Fluffy? Yes
– and it's all
my own hair

CHECK LIST

SIZE — Small – there is actually a tiny dog under all that fur

COLOUR — Many colours, most common are black, brown, orange

COAT TYPE — Long, straight, harsh overcoat with soft, fluffy undercoat

CARE GUIDE 🐾 🐾 🐾

CHARACTER TRAITS

These glamorous little dogs are much tougher than they look and can be very brave for their size. They are extremely affectionate and playful and form strong bonds with their owners. The Maltese is full of get-up-and-go and makes an adorable companion. They can be quick to bark and will try to take on larger dogs if this tendency is not kept in check.

CARE GUIDE

The beautiful, flowing locks of the Maltese do require daily attention. Their coats are not normally cut and need to be brushed every day to keep them tangle-free. They should have a bath every month or so and their eyes need to be regularly cleaned to stop staining of the hair. The hair is usually kept off the face with a tie. They are happy with short walks, but they are lively and do need playtime.

DID YOU KNOW?

Movie diva Elizabeth Taylor never went anywhere without her Maltese, Sugar, and even claimed the little pooch had spent more time in her bed than any of her husbands.

LOOKS FABULOUS IN…

The Maltese's amazing, long white locks make them very versatile style-wise and they are totally eye-catching when dressed in something special. They can wear exactly what you want them to – red, pink, blue, beige, tan and not forgetting leopard print. The list is endless. Malteses can carry off virtually any look and are especially dazzling if you get some sparkle in there somewhere.

"What a glamourpuss! My fellow diva Betty the Maltese is so beautiful and a real little princess."

Betty
MALTESE

Bring me my jewels!

CHECK LIST

SIZE small – a little bit of dog in a lot of coat

COLOUR White

COAT TYPE Long, straight and silky

CARE GUIDE

CHARACTER TRAITS

This sweet-natured pooch is one of the most popular breeds of small dog. Cheerful, friendly, affectionate, sociable and never aggressive, these spaniels love people and are fond of polite children. They have a melting expression, which is impossible not to love. They are not prone to excessive barking and are intelligent and easy to train.

CARE GUIDE

The Cav's coat is not particularly difficult to maintain but needs to be brushed several times a week to keep it in good condition. Their eyes need to be cleaned regularly. They are happy with a short walk but will also enjoy long country rambles. Highly adaptable, they will fit in with whatever you are doing but will soon become overweight if they don't get enough exercise. This breed suffers from a number of health problems, so it is important to find a responsible breeder.

DID YOU KNOW?

King Charles I and King Charles II both adored their tiny spaniels and this is how the breed got its name.

LOOKS FABULOUS IN…

Cavs are very popular in diva circles and most owners like to see them in fancy outfits, including little bow ties. The boys look really dashing in t-shirts or vest tops and the girls can definitely carry off a dress with a pleated skirt.

"Molly is such a popular pooch. Like all Cavalier King Charles spaniels, she is happy-go-lucky and great company. And who can resist those eyes?"

Molly

CAVALIER KING CHARLES SPANIEL

Yes, I really am as sweet as I look

CHECK LIST

SIZE Just the right size to share a sofa

COLOUR Black and tan; ruby; Blenheim (chestnut on white); tricolour (black, white, tan)

COAT TYPE Long, silky with feathering

CARE GUIDE

CHARACTER TRAITS

There are two types of Chinese crested – called hairless and powder puff – and both versions of this elegant little dog certainly make an impression. Cresteds are gentle and affectionate and they love their creature comforts. They become extremely attached to their owners and don't like to be left alone. They are bright, lively and playful and make charming companions.

CARE GUIDE

Chinese cresteds are naturally very clean and don't have a doggy smell. The hairless requires little grooming, but needs to be bathed frequently. The skin should be moisturised and needs to be protected in both cold and hot weather. They are particularly vulnerable to sunburn and also feel the cold, so they'll definitely need a coat in winter. The powder puff should be brushed every few days. They don't need a great deal of exercise but they do enjoy short walks and they like playing games and learning tricks.

DID YOU KNOW?

The Chinese crested dog was first seen in Britain in the 1830s as part of an exhibition of hairless dogs at London Zoo.

LOOKS FABULOUS IN…

The hairless crestie is a dog that definitely needs clothes. Because they haven't got any fur, it's a bit like dressing yourself. They will require a warm coat and jumper in winter and need to get used to wearing clothes from a young age. They can wear all sorts of different designs and look good in romper suits – these are great for keeping them warm at night.

"Gremlin the Chinese crested is the most unique poochie pal I've ever had. She looks amazing and has a personality to match – I just adore her!"

Gremlin

CHINESE CRESTED

Daahling... call my hairdresser — now!

CHECK LIST

SIZE small – just an armful of dog

COLOUR Black, grey, cream and white. Dark skin with pink patches when hairless

COAT TYPE Hairless variety has a silky mane, socks and tail. The powder puff has soft, long hair all over the body

CARE GUIDE

CHARACTER TRAITS

Shih-tzus are lively, sociable dogs who love being at the centre of family life. These charismatic characters are very independent and definitely know their own minds. Very much the companion dog, shih-tzus love being with people and get on with well-mannered children. They want to join in with whatever's going on but can be strong-willed and need patient training.

CARE GUIDE

The shih-tzu is a small dog with big hair and that wonderful coat needs a lot of attention, with daily brushing and a bath at least once a month or so. They can be trimmed or clipped and professional grooming is recommended. Shih's are active dogs and appreciate a good walk.

DID YOU KNOW?

Shih-tzu means 'lion dog' in Chinese and these dogs were once the companions of Buddhist monks.

LOOKS FABULOUS IN…

I personally think that shih's are adorably cute in pastel colours and soft fabrics, like fleece. This is another breed that looks great with 'up-dos' and bunches look fantastic.

"My friend Tia Maria is a cheeky, mischievous shih-tzu who absolutely has to be the centre of attention."

Tia Maria

SHIH-TZU

Yes, I look lovely. But can we play now?

CHECK LIST

SIZE Medium – just about lap-sized, even with all that hair

COLOUR Many colours, often with white blaze on forehead

COAT TYPE Long, flowing top coat with fairly thick undercoat

CARE GUIDE

"Baby Gracie the bulldog has an enormous character. She can be stubborn but she's a real softie and always good fun."

CHARACTER TRAITS

Despite their famously tough appearance, bulldogs are actually very gentle, calm dogs who make great family pets. They are loyal, dependable and very fond of their friends and family. Sometimes dignified, sometimes the clown, bulldogs are highly entertaining and inspire a great deal of affection in their owners. They can be a bit strong-willed and need to be properly trained.

CARE GUIDE

Bulldogs don't need much grooming but they should be brushed several times a week to remove dead hair. The folds of their skin should be kept clean to avoid infection. Because of their short noses, they are not very comfortable in hot weather and need access to shade when outside on a hot day. They don't need long walks but do have short bursts of energy, when they can move surprisingly quickly.

DID YOU KNOW?

Bulldogs were originally bred to fight bulls, but they became popular as companions after bull baiting was banned in 1835.

LOOKS FABULOUS IN…

Bulldogs can look a bit sullen, so it's a good idea to put them in cheerful colours. You could always try something outlandish, like a tutu – after all, our girl bulldogs are princesses, too. Boys can definitely work the tough look with studs and rivets on their clothes and accessories. You can really go to town with collars for these dogs – rows of sparkle are perfect for these show-offs. As they are quite muscular and strong, charms attached to their collar are easy for them to carry and won't make them feel like they're carting neck weights around. Perfect for that extra bling.

Baby Gracie

BULLDOG

serious? Wait till you see my comedy routine!

CHECK LIST

SIZE — Medium – short, but much too heavy for a handbag

COLOUR — Red, fawn, brindle, white or piebald (white with any of the above colours)

COAT TYPE — Fine, short, smooth

CARE GUIDE

CHARACTER TRAITS
The graceful Weimaraner is full of enthusiasm and loves being part of the family. Bred to be working dogs, these elegant pooches are intelligent and athletic and can become destructive if bored. They respond well to training but are likely to run rings round an inexperienced owner.

CARE GUIDE
The Weimaraner's coat is easy to care for and needs little more than a weekly brush to remove dead hairs. They can adapt to city life, but they are big dogs and need a fair amount of exercise, ideally at least two hours a day.

DID YOU KNOW?
Weimaraners are originally from Germany, where they were used for hunting.

LOOKS FABULOUS IN…
Now, you only need to look at these amazingly beautiful pooches to know that they are all class. Don't overload them with too many items – a stunning collar is all you need. They are so elegant that less is definitely more. They look an absolute dream in lilac, pink and turquoise.

"Daisy is so elegant. She is a Weimaraner and a lot bigger than some of my other friends but she's still a little flower."

Daisy
WEIMARANER

I know, I know. What can I say? I have great legs!

CHECK LIST

SIZE — Large – leggy, and far too big to sit on your lap

COLOUR — silver grey

COAT TYPE — short, smooth and sleek

CARE GUIDE

CHARACTER TRAITS
Originally bred to be a working dog, the schnauzer is lively and energetic and not really lapdog material. They are intelligent, friendly and love playing with their family and friends, but they do need to be well-trained because they can be on the stubborn side. They are natural guard dogs and may bark a lot.

CARE GUIDE
Although schnauzers are happy to live in a city, they need plenty of exercise to burn off all that energy and they love a good run in the countryside. They need to be combed several times a week and special attention needs to be paid to their faces and feet. Show schnauzers have bushy facial hair, which needs to be carefully groomed and washed. Pet schnauzers often have a trim to make them easier to care for. Their wiry coats should be hand-stripped two or three times a year by a professional groomer.

DID YOU KNOW?
The schnauzer gets its name from the German word for muzzle.

LOOKS FABULOUS IN…
When cut in the breed standard style, the schnauzer has an amazingly distinctive look with prominent eyebrows and beard. Because the coat is very short on the body and neck, schnauzers can really pull off a showy collar. They look stunning in red, pink and silver. Vest tops and body warmer-type clothing suit them best.

"My pal Ludo the schnauzer can be cheeky at times but he loves nothing more than snuggling in front of the fire with his human family."

Ludo

MINIATURE SCHNAUZER

Does my beard look big in this?

CHECK LIST

SIZE — Medium – knee-high, but too big to carry very far

COLOUR — salt and pepper, black and silver or black

COAT TYPE — Harsh, short and wiry

CARE GUIDE

MIX **IT UP!**

Not all dogs are pure-bred pedigrees and cross-breeds can have just as much flair and style as any diva.

A mixed-breed pooch can make a perfectly wonderful companion, but it's less easy to predict what their characters will be like or what type of care they will need. If you're getting a mixed-breed puppy, look carefully at the parents if possible – this will give you some idea what size your puppy is likely to be when they're fully grown and what coat type they may have. But remember, they can inherit characteristics from both parents and puppies in the same litter can look completely different.

I'm Ruby Roo, a Chihuahua and Jack Russell cross

My name's Betsey. I'm half Chihuahua, half Yorkie

These days, lots of people have a first generation cross – which is when two pedigrees are bred together. These are sometimes called designer dogs. Bringing a puppy into your life should be taken very seriously, so they mustn't be treated like designer shoes or handbags that are just a passing fashion fad. As irresistible as they may be, you mustn't choose your new puppy as if they were an accessory. These dogs are often given really cute names made up of a combination of the two breeds. The Yorkiepoo, for instance, is a Yorkshire terrier crossed with a poodle, and the puggle is a pug crossed with a beagle. Ideally, cross-breeds should inherit the best traits of both breeds, but remember they could just as easily end up with the worst qualities.

Some breeders charge a lot of money for these dogs, but no breeder should be in it for the profit, so be wary of anyone trying to sell a puppy for more than the cost of a standard pedigree pooch. As with any other dog, speak to the breeder and other owners to find out as much as possible about the cross-breed's character and needs before you commit.

PUPPY
LOVE

What's not to love about a puppy?
They are bundles of sweetness and
great fun. But they grow up very quickly
and those first days and months are
so precious. This is the beginning of a
beautiful friendship.

LITTLE **LOLA**

The day that Lola strutted into my life I wasn't really planning to get a puppy. When we went to see the litter, it was mainly to satisfy my little sister, who was desperate for a dog.

In the end, of course, we didn't leave empty-handed and I suddenly found myself with a new best friend. To be honest, I wasn't at all prepared for this precious new arrival in my life. We had nothing – nowhere for Lola to sleep, no bowls for water or food, not even a collar or harness.

I'm not saying this is the best way of going about things, but life doesn't always go to plan. Everything turned out fabulously for me and Lola but it's obviously a much better idea to be properly prepared for a new puppy. That means you have to go shopping, my favourite thing! Your newest family member will need something to eat, somewhere to sleep and something to travel home in. Before that, you need to do lots of research to make sure you're getting the right dog for you and that you know how to give them all the love and care you can.

Above all, you need to be certain that they have been born into a loving home and bred by people who really care about their dogs. Diva dogs are amazing, but they're not accessories, so please be sure to get them from a reputable breeder. The first time I saw Lola she was happily playing with her mum, brothers and sisters. The puppies were friendly and curious and they were clearly a special part of the family. I felt so much love from the owners that I just knew Lola's first few weeks of life had been as good as any dog could wish for. It was obvious that Caroline and Danny truly loved every puppy and we were at the house for ages, chatting and playing with the puppies.

People often ask me how to select a puppy from a litter – after all, they're all so cute, how do you choose just one? In my case, it was easy. Lola was the smallest and prettiest in the litter, but that's not the reason: the only way I can explain it is that Lola chose me. She attached herself to us more than the other puppies and I just knew she was the one.

Choosing Lola was the easy bit. Once I'd got her home, I had a lot to learn. This was my first ever dog and I didn't really know what to expect. She cried for a week. She had been taken from her family and it was heartbreaking, but I was certain I could console her and give her the best doggy life ever. I was surprised that such a tiny bundle of fur could have such a big personality and I adored her right from the start, but I was overprotective at times and didn't always know how to deal with practical issues. Fortunately, Lola has been a great teacher and I want to share some of her lessons with you.

The first time I met Lola, when she stole my heart

With Lola's first human parents – breeders Caroline and Danny

Lola's first ever photo shoot

In her first diva-style puppy bed

ola's first appearance on the V show 'A Different Breed'

My little princess at eight months

Lola's first night at home, snuggled in a blanket

ARE YOU REALLY, REALLY, REALLY **SURE YOU ARE READY FOR A PUPPY?**

Nothing in the world is lovelier than a puppy. Those tiny little paw pads, that cute little nose, that adorable snuggliness, their soft little bellies and their unbelievable loveableness.

Puppies are irresistible when they're playful and they're beyond cuteness when they're asleep. They even smell gorgeous.

But puppies also pee and poop and puke. They chew things, they whine, they get ill, they hate being left alone and they cost money. Are you really ready for all that? They also grow up into adult dogs very quickly and they live a long time – if you're lucky, your dog could live for at least 15 years, sometimes even longer (the oldest dog ever, according to the *Guinness World Records*, lived for an astonishing 29 years). Before you rush into getting a puppy, think carefully about what turns your life might take over the next 15 years or so.

If you're not put off by the idea of years of commitment, the sleepless nights, the wee, the muddy paw prints and the vet's bills, the next thing you need to think about is where to get a puppy from. Unfortunately, not all dog breeders have the best interests of their dogs at heart. Some people breed dogs purely because they want to make money. Every dog deserves to be loved to pieces from day one, so take some time to find a kind, responsible breeder.

SOME QUESTIONS TO ASK YOURSELF BEFORE YOU GET A PUPPY

- ♥ Will you be able to commit to a dog for its whole life?

- ♥ Do your work and social life give you enough free time to dedicate to a dog?

- ♥ Do you live somewhere suitable? If you rent, do you have permission to keep pets?

- ♥ What kind of holidays do you expect to have? What would you do with a dog while you're away?

- ♥ Does everyone in your family want a dog as much as you do? Would the new addition cause family disputes?

- ♥ Can you afford to pay vet's bills if your dog should become ill? Are you prepared to get pet insurance?

- ♥ Does anyone in your close family have an allergy to dogs?

One good place to start looking for a puppy is the Kennel Club, the people who organise the famous Crufts dog show. They have a 'find a puppy' service and an Assured Breeder Scheme. Breeders who sign up to the scheme are committed to raising healthy puppies in the best possible environment. It's also worth considering a dog from a charity rescue centre. They don't always have puppies available, but dogs from a rescue centre will always be assessed for character as well as vet-checked and vaccinated before you take them home.

Many people get their puppies through advertisements in local newspapers, shop windows, friends or other dog owners on internet forums. Although this can be fine, make sure your puppy is from a genuinely loving family before you buy. There are still some pet shops that sell dogs, but this is not a very good beginning for a young pup.

Dogs are family members, not tins of beans, and they shouldn't be bought and sold like groceries. Sometimes it can take quite a while to find the puppy that's just right for you – so be patient.

Wherever you get your new best friend from, it's essential that you see the puppy with their mother before you make a commitment. A responsible breeder will be happy to answer all your questions and should be knowledgeable about how to feed, groom and exercise that particular breed. If they really care about their dogs they will also be happy to offer you advice and support even after you've taken the youngster home with you.

You should expect your puppy to have already been to the vet's and to have had at least one course of vaccinations before they leave their family (puppies need two vaccinations – the first at eight weeks

and the second around 12 weeks). If your new addition is very small, injections may be postponed till they grow a little. Keep your pooch away from other dogs until they've had their needles. Be prepared for your pup to cry a little when they get vaccinated. Just be there to console your little one as any mum would. I had Lola microchipped at the same time. Even though I'm an overprotective fur-baby mum, I knew it was worth putting her through the discomfort of another needle to keep her safe.

Many breeders will give you a free pet insurance plan for the first few weeks. Insurance is very important as vet's bills can be extremely costly. I strongly recommend that you look into pet insurance as soon as possible; we wouldn't want a poorly pup without the funds to make them feel better. Lola sadly had an injury when she was just six months old and the vet's bill came to £1,500. It was definitely a costly way to realise just how essential pet insurance is.

WHAT IS A PUPPY FARM?

Puppy farms are horrible places where dogs are bred purely for profit. They are kept in terrible conditions, sometimes left to fester in their own mess, starving, dehydrated, ill-treated and shown no love or affection.

Female dogs have litter after litter, which can lead to horrific injuries and illnesses. The mums are left tired, exhausted and in pain. Puppies are often taken from their mothers far too early. These people know that small dogs are in demand and sometimes tell new owners that the pups are older than they actually are so they can sell them quickly and before they are ready to leave their mother (which should not be before about eight weeks). This cruel business results in unhealthy, unhappy dogs.

People who run puppy farms can be very devious and often pose as responsible breeders, so it's not always easy to spot them. There are a few warning signs to look out for before you get your puppy:

♥ If more than one breed of dog is listed in the same advertisement, the dogs may be puppy-farmed.

♥ If a breeder won't let you see the puppy with their mum, you should be very suspicious. The breeder may give you lots of convincing excuses, but you should not buy a puppy unless you can see its mother.

♥ Don't buy a puppy from a pet shop – many of these come from puppy farms and all dogs should start their lives in a loving family home.

♥ Never buy a pup because you feel sorry for them or you think you are rescuing them; you will only encourage the breeder to keep producing poorly pups.

♥ Never buy a puppy because it seems like a bargain. If a dog costs less than the market value, the deal is probably too good to be true – the puppy may even be stolen.

♥ NEVER agree to buy a puppy from the back of a van in a car park – this is how puppy farmers and their dealers often operate.

BEFORE YOUR PUPPY
COMES HOME

Puppy's homecoming is a big occasion. You'll probably have butterflies in your tummy and have been counting down the weeks, days and even hours till this day.

You'll want to be prepared so get yourself some essential poochie goodies and puppy-proof your home to make sure the new arrival is safe and can't do too much damage.

Remember that leaving home is a really big deal for your little baby – they're about to say goodbye to everything they've ever known and loved. This is also the beginning of your new friendship and your first few days and weeks together are an opportunity for you to bond.

If possible, visit the breeder's home at least twice, so you can really get to know your new dog. It's also a good idea to leave an old t-shirt that you have worn for the youngster to sleep on so that they become familiar with your scent. You could take along some toys, too.

PUPPY'S HOMECOMING SHOPPING LIST – ABSOLUTE ESSENTIALS

- ♥ Travel crate or carrier
- ♥ Bedding
- ♥ Food and water bowls
- ♥ Puppy food
- ♥ Puppy toys (chew toys and cuddle toys)

HOW TO PUPPY-PROOF
YOUR HOUSE

Even the tiniest puppy can be destructive or put themselves in danger. Look at your home from their eye-level.

Please look after me!

PUPPY-PROOF YOUR HOUSE

Is there anything potentially hazardous that a puppy could reach? Could they get hold of anything that's really precious to you? Puppies will have a go at chewing almost anything, so you'll need to have a good tidy-up before the homecoming.

Here are a few safety steps you can take before you bring the new arrival home:

♥ Prepare one area of the house, such as the kitchen, where you can safely confine your puppy

♥ Puppy pens are a fab way to keep them safe and out of harm's way

♥ Bells can be added to a puppy's collar, so you'll always know where they are

♥ Use a dog gate to stop them trying to climb the stairs or get into other rooms in the house

♥ Remember to close front and back doors to stop your curious pup from venturing out

♥ Tidy away anything that could be chewed – especially valuable things like mobile phones or your favourite shoes

♥ Move house plants out of reach (some plants are poisonous)

♥ Remove anything that could easily be knocked over, such as vases and ornaments

♥ Put hazardous things like bleach or medicines well out of reach

♥ Don't leave food anywhere your puppy might be able to reach it, especially chocolate, which can be fatal for dogs

♥ If you have a garden, put any chemicals or tools out of reach

♥ Be aware of poisonous plants and shrubs and creepy-crawlies such as slugs and snails, which can carry the life-threatening lungworm

♥ Block any gaps in your garden and make sure that your pup cannot fit underneath fences or gates

HOW TO BE THE PERFECT
PUPPY PARENT

Leave your secure carrier and a blanket with the breeder a few days before you collect your little one so they can get used to it.

BRINGING YOUR PUPPY HOME

A carrier with a snuggly blanket is like a little mobile kennel which should make your puppy feel comfortable and secure.

It's best if the puppy doesn't eat for a few hours before the journey; lots of puppies are travel sick on their first car journey. If you have to travel a long way, take a rest stop after about two hours and give them a drink of water. Above all, drive carefully – a smooth journey will help put them at ease.

GETTING INTO A FEEDING ROUTINE

Ask your breeder what food the puppy has been eating and stick to that to begin with because a sudden change of diet may cause an upset stomach. Youngsters should be fed up to four times a day until about 10 weeks. Reduce this to three meals at around 10 weeks and drop down to twice a day at about four months old. Try to stick to regular meal times as this will help with house-training.

Make sure that you do not feed your little one too many treats as they can get very upset tummies quite easily. If you do give them a treat, make sure it's a puppy treat – adult ones will be too rich and you may have a few unexpected surprises on your floors…Oops!

PUPPY'S FIRST FEW DAYS

Your first few days together are a very exciting time and naturally you'll be thrilled to bits with your tiny new pooch. You'll be tempted to spend every minute fussing over them but remember that, just like human babies, puppies need lots of rest and sleep.

If you want your little baby to grow up into a well-adjusted adult you need to set a few ground rules right from the start. Don't give in to their every whim or pick them up at every whine or whimper. Your puppy needs to get used to not having your full attention all the time. This is very important if you plan on leaving your new addition for periods of time in the future. Spoilt pups can get separation anxiety and, although it's very hard to ignore them, you don't want problems later on. I adore all my furkids and they are lucky enough to be able to go everywhere with me, but most dogs will have to be left alone for some of the time.

My pooches have always had free reign of our house and they have a lovely plush bed in my room. If you're happy to have an adult dog sleeping in the bedroom or even on the bed, that's completely up to you. But if you don't want this to happen then you need to get your puppy used to sleeping apart from you as soon as possible. You can begin by putting their bed inside the bedroom and then move it further away from yours over a couple of nights. Your puppy will probably cry during the night to begin with – but they will get used to it. To help them settle in, make sure they have a comfortable bed where they feel safe and secure and give them a toy to keep them occupied. If they whine, try to ignore them (this is really, really hard but will help them settle in more quickly). To help them relax, you can buy a plug-in DAP (Dog Appeasing Pheromone) diffuser that releases female hormones. This calms your little one by making them feel that mummy is close by.

Of course you'll be proud of your adorable fur-bundle and will want to show them off to the whole world, but don't overwhelm them. Remember your pup needs time to adapt – so the introductions, the puppy parties, the meet-and-greets and the trips to the puppy café or the local hip hang-out can wait until your pup is properly settled into their new home.

You may have chosen a name way ahead of actually getting your pup, but sometimes you need to get to know a dog before you find the right name. It doesn't really matter what you call your dog, but ideally it should be short and not too embarrassing to shout across a park. It's important to decide on a name as soon as possible because it will help with training.

GETTING HANDS-ON

Right from the beginning you should be doing a regular five-minute inspection at least once a week so you can get to know your dog and learn to identify anything that isn't quite right. See the grooming pages for tips on how to do this. This will also make your puppy comfortable with being handled, making it less traumatic when it's time to visit the groomer or the vet. The earlier you start, the more tolerant your dog will be of being handled.

If your pooch is going to be professionally groomed, book the first grooming appointment at around 15 weeks old (they'll need to have all their jabs before they go).

LEAVING YOUR DOG ALONE

If it was up to your puppy, you'd never be apart. Dogs are pack animals and they don't like to be left alone. Many diva dogs are fortunate to spend lots of time with their mums and dads and are taken to events, to work or on shopping trips. However, if you have to leave your little one, it's important that they learn to be happy without you. You can start doing this while you're still in the house. Put them in their safe place (a confined area, playpen or crate) and move to somewhere they can't see you. Try to ignore any whining. Gradually increase the amount of time you leave them alone. Once they are happy with this, you can start to leave the house for short periods of time. When you come home, try not to make a big fuss of them straight away – I know it's hard, but it really is for the best. Wait for them to calm down before you say hello and give them big snuggles.

WHAT'S MY NAME?

Puppies can learn their names really quickly. All you need to do is crouch down, open your arms and call them to you with a happy tone of voice. They will naturally run towards you. Reward them with treats and cuddles. Do this a couple of times a day. Within a matter of days, your puppy should be responding to their name. Then you'll be able to start teaching them even more tricks.

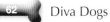

TIME TO TAKE
ON THE WORLD

Once the little one has settled in, it's time to make introductions. Your young puppy is totally open to new experiences.

Puppies are curious and trusting and eager to try new things. Once they get to 12 or 13 weeks, they become more suspicious and wary, so it's important that they encounter as many experiences as possible before they hit this phase. This process is called socialisation and involves introducing them to all sorts of people, other pets and things that move and make a noise. When I first got Lola, I wanted to keep her all to myself and I didn't realise how important socialisation was. Now I recognise that I wasn't doing her any favours.

Dogs that are poorly socialised as puppies may be frightened of unfamiliar things for the rest of their lives, so make the most of this short window to prepare them for whatever life has to throw at them. You can start with things in the home, such as washing machines, vacuum cleaners, hairdryers, cats, children, friends and family. When your puppy is fully vaccinated, they're ready to face the world with all its noises, smells and new sensations. They'll need to get used to cars, buses, shopping trolleys, skateboards and all sorts of things that we come across in our day-to-day lives.

A puppy class or training club is an ideal place for your little one to make new doggy friends. Many

vet's surgeries run puppy classes and they can be really enjoyable for both of you. I loved going to our sessions and it was a fantastic opportunity to swoon over the other adorable furbabies.

BASIC TRAINING

It's never too early to start teaching your dog some basic tricks. Spending time together in this way is fun and helps you both to bond. The very easiest thing to teach a dog is to sit. All you have to do is to hold a small treat in front of their nose. Most dogs will naturally sit when you do this. Repeat a couple of times and then introduce the 'sit' command. Very soon poochie will sit when you ask.

Training is not about making a dog obedient for the sake of it. Asking them to sit or stay before a meal or a treat strengthens communication between you and makes them more responsive. Dogs are highly intelligent animals and they enjoy having something to do. If you want your puppy to grow into a well-behaved adult and, most importantly of all, to come back to you when they're off the lead, it's a good idea to get into the habit of training them for a few minutes a day, several times a week. Puppies, like children, have a short attention span, so little and often is best. You can also train

them not to do things like jumping up at people or leaping on furniture. Never punish them for getting it wrong – you will only put them off the whole idea of education. The secret to a well-trained dog is reward, reward, reward. They love you and will do anything to make you happy, so show your appreciation with small, healthy treats and lots of love and praise.

TIME TO MEET THE VET

Your puppy should already have visited a vet at least once with the breeder to have their first vaccinations, but it's still a good idea to take them for a check-up as soon as possible. Your little one doesn't yet associate the vet with horrible things and this first visit is part of the socialisation process. If you don't already have another pet, this is also a chance for you to meet the vet. One day, sooner or later, your dog's health and well-being will depend on decisions you make with your vet, so it's important that you trust them.

PUPPY'S FIRST TRIP TO THE VET

Even if nothing at all seems to be wrong with your puppy, they should go to the vet's for a check-up. Your vet will:

♥ Give them a thorough check-up to make sure everything is as it should be

♥ Give you advice on vaccination against potentially fatal diseases such as distemper, parvovirus and hepatitis

♥ Give you advice on preventing parasites such as ticks, fleas and worms

♥ Offer to microchip your puppy so they can be traced if they get lost

♥ Discuss the option of neutering

♥ Answer any questions you have on any aspects of your puppy's well-being

Imagine how exciting the world must be from a puppy's point of view. So many new sounds, smells, tastes and textures and fun things to try out. Every puppy should feel safe, secure and loved enough to enjoy this wonderful new world.

What's the weather like up there?

HOUSE-TRAINING
YOUR PUPPY

Let's be honest, dogs don't exactly have a reputation for cleanliness. But, in actual fact, they really don't like to mess in their own sleeping area.

Your puppy's instincts to keep a clean bed will make it fairly easy to house-train them with a bit of patience. The best way to house-train a dog quickly is to avoid accidents in the first place – prevention is better than cure. An eight-week-old puppy needs to wee about eight times a day, and it's your duty to make sure they have access to somewhere suitable to go. Of course, accidents will happen, but if you invest some time and effort in the first couple of weeks, your pup should soon get the hang of it.

A puppy may want to wee at any time, but there are particular times when they are more likely to need to go: when they wake up, after a meal and after an exciting event (such as playing a game or the arrival of a visitor). You might find that you'll need to go to bed late and get up early for the first couple of weeks to avoid accidents. It's important to reward your puppy for getting it right; lots of love and praise and a small titbit will get the message home that you're pleased with your pooch.

PAPER-TRAINING
People used to use newspaper to house-train their dogs, but these days you can buy special training pads – which look a bit like a flat nappy. These are much better than newspaper because they are more absorbent. You can also get training pads that have a scent to attract the pup to wee on it.

When your new arrival first comes home, confine them to a fairly small area (kitchens are good for this because they usually have easy-to-clean floors). This will keep your pup safe and make it much easier to house-train them.

For the first few days, cover the area with pads. Very soon, your pup will identify a particular spot where they prefer to do their business. Then you can reduce the number of pads you put down to two or three in this area.

Put them on the pad after waking, eating or playing or if they look like they need to go. Reward them every time they use the pad.

CRATE-TRAINING
A crate is a basket or carrier where a puppy can be confined at times when supervision is not possible. Crate-training follows the same principle as paper-

training but, as puppies will generally not go to the toilet in their crate, this method reduces the chances of accidents at those moments when you are not able to keep an eye on them. When you take your puppy out of the crate, you can put them on a pad or in the garden and reward them if they go.

This can be a very effective way of house-training, but you should only ever use it for short periods of time. The crate should be a safe, happy place – never shut your little one in a crate as a punishment for naughty behaviour.

If you decide to choose this method, introduce the crate slowly over a few days. At first, leave the crate door open and put a cosy blanket and some toys in it. Putting a few biscuits inside the crate will also help your puppy associate it with happy things. When your puppy seems comfortable in the crate, shut the door for just a minute or two and then reward them. Then gradually increase the time they spend in the crate.

OUTDOOR TRAINING

Remember that when your puppy first arrives they will probably not be fully vaccinated, so they can't go outside your home. However, if you have a garden you may prefer to train them to go to the toilet outside from the beginning.

You can do this with the same method as paper-training. Keep them confined to a small area (or crate) and take them into the garden frequently so they have a chance to go in the right place.

To start with, try to take them outside every hour during the day and evening. If they go to the toilet, reward them with praise and treats. You should find that your little dear soon learns where to go.

You can gradually increase the time between garden visits, but keep taking your puppy outside after waking, eating and playing until they are fully house-trained. For the first few weeks or so, it's going to mean some early mornings for you to avoid accidents.

DON'T PUNISH YOUR PUPPY (BUT DO CLEAN UP!)

Never punish your dog for accidents. Dogs don't know that weeing on the carpet is bad.

If you start shouting because you've found a puddle your puppy won't understand why you're angry. All they know is that you're being scary. Some people believe their dogs 'look' guilty when they've done something wrong. But it's not really guilt, it's fear.

Punishing your dog may actually make house-training more difficult and will damage your relationship. Dogs respond much better to rewards than punishments.

If they do have an accident in the house, make sure you clean it up thoroughly. Dogs have an incredible sense of smell and they are more likely to wee somewhere that already smells of wee.

HOW DO YOU KNOW WHEN YOUR PUPPY NEEDS TO GO?

One of the secrets of successful house-training is spotting when your dog needs to go before they actually do, so that you can whizz them over to their training pad or out into the garden.

A dog that needs to go to the toilet may start sniffing around more than usual, pace up and down, whine, look worried and be unable to settle down. If you see this behaviour, act quickly to avoid accidents.

CARING FOR
YOUR DIVA DOG

4

As you've probably worked out by now, I think dogs are just the most awesome thing in the world. There's loads of evidence that it's good for us to have them around – they reduce our stress levels, keep us fitter and make us a whole lot happier. They do so much for us, it's only right that we treat them with respect. No matter how cute your poochie poo is (and I'm sure they're absolutely adorable), they are dogs first and foremost. Finding out about what makes them tick makes it easier for us to get along.

LET'S **TALK**

Dogs, of course, can't speak and we're not much good at woofing, either. Yet, over the thousands of years we've been living together, dogs and people have learnt how to communicate amazingly well.

They may not be able to understand our actual words, but dogs are highly sensitive to our tone of voice and our moods. I sometimes think that my pooches actually understand me better than anyone (except, perhaps, my mother – she can definitely read my thoughts).

I'm not too proud to admit that I often use baby-speak with my little ones. Lola is 'Lola Lollikins' and she has 'din-dins' and goes 'beddy-byes' after she's been 'wee wees'. I also often find myself telling them what I'm doing – 'Dinner's not going to be long', I'll say, or, 'We'll go for a walk as soon as mummy's finished her tea'. A favourite phrase of mine to get their attention is, 'What's mummy got?' Even if they don't understand the words, I'm absolutely sure they find it reassuring to hear a gentle voice. Dogs have a much better sense of hearing than we do, so shouting in their presence is something I would never do. They can't understand that it's really your other half you're angry with, they just sense something is wrong – and that's scary.

Our furbabies are constantly in tune with us, watching, listening and sensing how we feel. Believe me, if you're having a bad hair day, they

will know all about it. On many occasions, I've had down days when my hectic life has taken its toll and I've needed to stay in bed just to recharge my batteries. Whenever this happens, my babies stay with me all day huddled on my bed. This is unconditional love in action.

But what about us? How much do we understand about what our little babies are trying to say? Dogs compensate for not having words by using their whole bodies to speak, as well as an extensive repertoire of noises. I never did very well at languages when I was at school – I think '*Bonjour, je m'appelle Louise*' is the extent of my linguistic skills – but spending so much time with my little ones has made me pretty good at doggy-speak.

Lola is very good at communicating. She speaks with her eyes, as most of my furkids do. She will always tell me what she wants by whining a little then looking at me and then looking at what it is that she wants. Normally, it's her favourite bear, which she's had since she was a baby. It has missing eyes and a broken nose but she hates to be separated from it and has no problem communicating this fact.

She is the only one who will alert me on the rare occasions that their drinking water has run out. She does a high-pitched yap in short bursts. I'm straight in there, pouring out their fresh spring water and, of course, apologising to them – bad mummy!

As leader of the pack, and my original diva dog, Lola is definitely boss. She will stand proud and bark to protect me and her furry siblings if she senses danger. Usually, it's just the postman, but I still take comfort in the fact that my babies will alert me to any potential danger.

The best moment for me is when I come home and see my babies go crazy. They start crying at the door as soon as they hear my car pull up in the drive. They give me the best doggy loves ever, which tells me they are happy.

Generally speaking, you know you have a happy dog if their ears are relaxed and their tails are wagging. If they want some attention they will often dance around in front of you and pat you with a paw. Sometimes they will roll over on their backs – a clear invitation for a tummy rub and a bit of fuss.

Scared dogs tend to flatten their ears, lower their tails and hunch their bodies. They may also raise their hackles – the hairs along the back of the neck and spine. Raised hackles can also be a sign of aggression. Bad-tempered dogs may growl, bare their teeth and stiffen their bodies. Nervous or anxious dogs often look around in a quick, darting fashion and lick their lips.

A waggy tail is something most of us associate with doggy happiness, but that's not always the case. Excitable, enthusiastic tail-wagging usually does mean a pup is feeling happy and friendly, but if a dog is slowly wagging a lowered tail, it could mean they are feeling defensive and don't want to be approached. Yawning is another odd one. You'd think a yawning dog must just be sleepy. In fact, dogs often yawn when they are afraid or feeling uncertain about something. Of course, sometimes a yawning pup is just dog tired.

When you share your life with a dog, you quickly learn their language and they are experts at teaching us to understand (and obey!) their instructions. They whine when they want attention or food or to be let out and they bark to warn us about day-to-day dangers, like postmen or the neighbour's cat. Yelping or whimpering could mean your little one is in pain and this is something you really should listen to.

IT'S **PLAYTIME!**

The play bow is one of the cutest things that doggies do. This is when they lower the front half of their bodies, bend their elbows, pop their little bums in the air and wag their tails furiously.

This pose is your dog's way of telling us (and other dogs) that they want to play. They lower themselves to the ground to make it clear that they are not being aggressive, they just want a spot of rough and tumble.

This is a good time to get out some toys and give your playful pooch a bit of a work-out. A tug rope or throw toy will keep you both entertained. Puppies are particularly playful, but adult dogs also enjoy playing games, often even into old age. They enjoy playing with toys which appeal to their natural instincts to chase, pounce, shake and chew. Dogs of all ages also like soft, cuddly toys to snuggle up with. Dogs are very bright and like a challenge, so some of the interactive toys now on the market, such as doggy puzzles or play gyms, can be a great way to satisfy a diva dog's demanding ways.

Avoid giving your pooch toys with small parts that could be swallowed and don't buy children's toys, as they are not safe for dogs. Luckily, there are lots of lovely toys available these days that are specially designed with the pampered pooch in mind. Even so, it's always best to supervise your pup with all toys… just in case.

PLAY NICELY

Diva dogs don't snarl – that's just rude, undignified behaviour. A little play growl can be cute. They might growl while playing a game of tug, for example, all in fun. But growling possessively over toys, food or sofa space is so not cool. If this happens, it probably means they're getting too big for their boots and you may need to set some boundaries to get them back on track to being your friend, not your boss. As much as we want to pamper, love and spoil our little ones, we always have to be the pack leader or they can develop behavioural problems. The truly brilliant poochie parent knows when it's time to stick to the rules.

TOY BOX
There are some fabulously fun dog toys
available these days that will both entertain
your little diva and amuse you, too.

PART OF **THE FAMILY**

Dogs are naturally sociable creatures and they love the safe, secure feeling they get from being with their pack.

Dogs can be very open-minded about who is considered part of their family and will usually give a cheery welcome to friends, family and doggy pals. That doesn't mean they will always take to new people straight away and introductions shouldn't be rushed. Some dogs will feel threatened if a new person enters their territory and may bark at them at first. Dogs need to observe, sniff and generally check someone out before they are admitted to the pack.

Lola can be more accepting than my other three furry ones. She adores a bit of stroking and fuss and she loves being the centre of attention. The other three are not so great at accepting new people into our family and they tend to have a competition to see who can bark the loudest when anyone comes round. This is mainly through uncertainty and nerves – my little ones have led sheltered lives. This is why I want to give you some advice about raising your poochies in the best way possible. You can learn from my mistakes and, believe me, socialising your dogs from an early age is vitally important. If a puppy is well-socialised early on, they are more likely to be well-mannered adults who will love the opportunity to expand their social circle.

MULTIPLE-DOG FAMILIES

I started off with one dog and soon ended up with four, and I haven't ruled out the possibility of more – who knows? I've never regretted expanding my family for a minute and it's so cute to have your own mini-pack. They look out for each other and my second eldest, Lulu, is definitely the mother of the pack. She will go and search for the others if any of them are missing when I call.

Owners of small dogs often have more than one because they don't take up much room and they tend to get on so well together. However, having more than one dog is a serious commitment and you have to be prepared to spend time with them as individuals as well as a group. We don't want any little noses pushed out, so be sure that you always devote extra time to your existing babies when a new pup joins the family.

A growing family can be expensive, too. Each dog will need their own equipment, annual vaccinations and insurance policy. I feel sad when I hear strories about owners who just love animals so much that they keep welcoming more, but can't afford to look after them properly. Be absolutely certain that you can care for each furry one financially as well as emotionally.

In most cases, I wouldn't recommend getting two puppies from the same litter. I say this because it's very difficult to train and socialise two pooches at the same time and there's a risk that they will be more attached to each other than to you. Also, bear in mind size, breed and temperament. All mine are Yorkies from different litters but the same breeder, so they are perfect for each other, but a dainty pooch could be injured or frightened by a large, boisterous dog.

If you do decide to get a second (or third, or fourth) dog, initial introductions need to be carefully handled. The new arrival may be seen as an unwelcome intruder and be given the cold-shoulder to begin with. Don't leave them alone until things have settled down and make sure both existing and new dogs have a safe place where they can get some quiet 'me' time.

It will help if you avoid creating situations where they may become competitive. Don't put their food bowls too close to each other and watch them to make sure nobody steals. Things will go more smoothly if your little darlings don't have to compete for sleeping space, toys or your attention. Only get more than one dog if you've got lots of love to give. My clients and doggy friends often tell me they worry about getting another pooch in case their first furkid gets jealous and feels left out. I had exactly the same thoughts. Lola had been my shadow for over a year and I wasn't sure she would like sharing the limelight. In the end, it turned out to be the best decision I ever made and I'm now truly a pooch addict. Luckily, dogs like other dogs, so with a little effort and patience, you should soon have a very happy little family.

DOGS AND CHILDREN

Most children love dogs, especially tiny, cute ones. In fact, 'dog' is very often one of the first words a baby learns to say. Unfortunately, the feeling is not always mutual. Small children don't necessarily understand the difference between a toy and a real dog and they may not realise how fragile a tiny pooch can be. Obviously, it depends on the individual child, but in most cases I don't recommend tiny, diva dog breeds for families with small children. A dog can't say, 'Hey, baby, stop pulling me around', they can only react by getting irritated and possibly snapping at the child. This is something that no parent wants to happen. Children can also injure little pooches quite easily because their bones and joints are so delicate.

I missed out on having dogs when I was a child, but I do appreciate that pet ownership can be hugely beneficial to children and can teach them a lot about kindness and responsibility. Both the child's safety and the dog's welfare are vitally important so here are a few points to consider if there are children in your dog's life:

- Never get a dog just because a child wants one
- A child can't be expected to take responsibility for a dog's well-being
- Teach children how to handle dogs respectfully and gently
- Children should never stare at dogs or approach them while they are sleeping
- Don't let children eat food near dogs or touch a dog while they are eating
- Never allow a child to tease or play roughly with a dog
- Socialise your dog to be relaxed around children

ESTABLISHING HOUSE RULES

Diva dogs are often spoilt rotten, loved to pieces and treated like kings and queens of the castle. You'll want to do everything you can to make them feel special. In return, they should be well-mannered enough to respect a few house rules. Getting home to chewed shoes, shredded cushions or torn up mail can put a strain on even the closest of friendships.

The best way to deal with doggy naughtiness is to stop it happening in the first place. Don't lead them into temptation by giving them the opportunity to misbehave. Keep the house tidy, don't leave food anywhere they could reach it and don't leave tempting, chewable items like slippers lying about. Make sure they have plenty of opportunity to go to the toilet in the right place, so you don't come home to puddles…or worse.

I really must own up to the fact that my diva dogs have always been very well-behaved. I know it's rare, but I've never had eaten shoes or chewed table legs. I know one pooch who actually ate through the plasterboard in the kitchen and had white poop for a week afterwards. Luckily, my four amazing furry kids have never done anything like that.

Small dogs are generally less destructive than bigger dogs – mainly because it's easier to keep things out of their reach and they're not strong enough to open doors and cupboards or knock things over. But diva dogs are particularly good at getting their own way. It's amazing how quickly a furbaby can train a human to pick them up and put them on a cushion on the sofa. My dogs go wherever they want, so I'm hardly going to insist on a 'dogs off the furniture' policy. They have even trained me to pick them up to put them on the sofa, even though they actually have little steps to help them get on to one of their favourite snuggle spots.

What's important is that you are consistent. It's no use deciding that your little furry isn't allowed on the sofa one minute and then putting them on your lap the next because you feel like a cuddle while you're watching a weepy film. Nor is it helpful if other members of the family apply different rules. When it comes to doggy discipline, everyone should be singing from the same hymn sheet – it's just not fair on the little one if the rules of the game keep changing.

GETTING AWAY **FROM IT ALL**

Because of my hectic lifestyle, I don't get away on holiday very often. When I do, I leave my little ones with mummy diva.

Having my mum doggy-sit means I know they'll be cared for properly. If you don't have anyone to leave your dog with, you need to think carefully about what's going to happen to them while you're soaking up the sun and sipping cosmopolitans.

Boarding kennels are an option, but personally I'd find it very difficult to leave my furbabies with strangers. If you are considering kennels, make sure you visit first and get recommendations from other owners. Some kennels specialise in looking after smaller dogs, which is a great idea because it could be very intimidating for your little one if they are suddenly surrounded by large, noisy dogs. There are a few luxury boutique hotels for pooches around – these are generally not cheap, but our little ones are worth it!

If you cannot find kennels that you feel comfortable with there is always the option of a house/dog sitter who could stay in your home. This helps by keeping your dog in their own surroundings and may reduce the stress of being apart from their human parents. Do remember to research very thoroughly and take up references if you are considering allowing someone into your home.

Of course, you could always go on holiday together. Dogs – especially one or two well-behaved little ones – are welcome at many camping sites, caravan parks, B&Bs, hotels and holiday cottages throughout the UK. If you're not into camping or caravanning, you could always check into the hotel chain, Hilton. Me and Lola love them and thanks to Ms Hilton and her love of pooches most of their hotels are very welcoming to our diva dogs – just check before you go.

Before booking any holiday accommodation, make sure the place really is dog-friendly. Ask if there are restrictions on where your furry travelling companion can go and if there is somewhere nearby where they can exercise. A word of warning: my diva doggy friends tell me it's very hard to find somewhere that will let you take two or more dogs.

If you are travelling with your dog, make sure you pack a poochie suitcase with all your little friend's bedding, feeding bowls and favourite toys. Take your doggy carrier with you, too, so you have somewhere safe to put them.

Thanks to the Pet Passport, it's now possible for our furry friends to go abroad, but there's quite a lot of paperwork involved. Me and Lola travelled to Ireland and we were very lucky that the cabin crew seated me directly next to my baby so I could make sure she was okay. Even so, I don't think it

I'm packed and ready to go!

was the most pleasant experience for her, but I was adamant that my princess wasn't going in the luggage hold – as if!

If you are going abroad, your little one will need to be vaccinated for rabies, as well as all the usual jabs, and you have to wait for this to take effect. It's a lovely idea to take your best pal on holiday with you, but it's not without its drawbacks. Some countries, especially in southern Europe, have parasites that we don't have here and our dogs haven't built up any resistance to these unfamiliar bugs. Also, if you're going somewhere hotter than home, your pooch may not enjoy the heat as much as you do. If you are considering taking poochie abroad, your vet will be able to talk you through all the pros and cons of foreign travel.

DEALING WITH
COMMON PROBLEMS

Even the dearest darling can be troublesome at times, but most doggy difficulties can be nipped in the bud before they become a real problem. Understanding your dog's behaviour is the first step.

SEPARATION ANXIETY

Although dogs are sociable animals, a truly contented pooch will be happy to be alone some of the time. If a dog becomes very unhappy and agitated when they are left alone, they may be suffering from separation anxiety. This can be really upsetting for you and your dog and can result in excessive barking, destructiveness and messing in the house.

To prevent this problem occurring in the first place, your precious pooch needs to learn to be without you some of the time from the very beginning. Separation anxiety is a condition we can create just by loving them so much that we never leave them alone. The trouble is that we don't always give them the chance to become independent, confident little characters who are comfortable in their own company.

If your little one demands attention, don't always respond straight away. Try to ignore them until they settle down – then you can make a big fuss. It might seem really, really cute when you get a big barky welcome every time you arrive home, but it's best to wait until they've calmed down before you say hello. If they are following you around all the time it might seem like devotion, but it can also be a sign of insecurity. They're following you because they're worried about what will happen if they can't see you. This isn't a healthy situation, so try to discourage this. Lots of super-cosy comfort zones will help your pooch find somewhere they can relax without worrying about what you're up to every minute of the day. If you help them to feel comfortable on their own when you are in the house, it'll be a lot easier for them when you have to go out. Apart from anything else, even the loveliest dog in the world can get on your nerves if they're constantly whining for attention or pawing at you. I'm a devoted diva dog owner, yet I still appreciate some dog-free moments now and again.

EXCESSIVE BARKING

Barking is part of normal dog behaviour and is one of the ways in which they communicate. Lola will sometimes have barking moments during the day but it's usually just to let me know there is someone near the house. This is perfectly normal and you should expect your dog to bark some of the time. If you want a dog that never barks, get a cat. That said, excessive barking is not only annoying to you and your neighbours, it can be a sign that your pooch is not as happy as they should be. Dogs may bark because they are bored, defending their territory, trying to get attention or feeling scared or insecure. A dog who feels safe, has a toy to occupy themselves with and who feels relaxed in their surroundings is less likely to become a problem barker. Dogs sometimes bark because they're really excited and want to have some fun, but if their barking is persistent, prolonged or aggressive, you'll need to investigate what it is that's going wrong for them and how you can help them feel more secure.

AGGRESSION

A diva dog should never be aggressive, it's just not the sort of behaviour we want in our little loves. Nevertheless, even the tiniest pooch may growl and bare their teeth if they feel uncomfortable or threatened. Tiny divas are unlikely to do anyone much damage, so it's easy to overlook this behaviour. Still, it's rude to snap or growl and you won't get invited to doggy socials if your companion can't be polite. After all, it's so not cool to be a brawler.

It's not the dog's fault – it never is – so we have to blame the parents, I'm afraid. Early socialisation will help them to face the world without fear and make them less likely to develop aggressive tendencies. Small puppies will naturally bite while they're playing. Because this doesn't hurt, it's easy to laugh it off and let them carry on. What you actually should do is yelp and pretend you're in pain. This way your little one will learn that you are a fragile thing and that they shouldn't bite, even in play.

You may also make your fur-bundle defensive and snappy if you are an overprotective mummy. Small dogs whose every whim is indulged get used to having their own way and may not take kindly to anyone else who gets too near their mum or dad. If your precious one growls at other people when you're holding them, put them on the floor. Don't pick them up again until they stop making such a silly fuss. They'll soon learn that they need to behave nicely if they want to stay in the lap of luxury. If your perfectly placid, gentle pooch suddenly develops aggressive tendencies, there may be an underlying medical cause and you should get them checked out by a vet.

Many owners of small dogs worry that their little babies might be attacked by another dog. This is a really tricky one and I know how anxious I've been when a big, bouncy dog comes striding across the park towards my pooches. It's tempting to scoop up your furkids at the first sight of potential trouble, but this could make them more fearful. Remember that your pooch picks up on your anxiety and you could turn them into a bundle of nerves. It's important that they have really good recall (see page 122) so you can get them back quickly if you do see a dog who doesn't look too friendly.

Most of the time, dogs can sort it out among themselves and small dogs are often quick to stand up for themselves. However, always be vigilant for signs of aggression in other dogs. If another dog's behaviour is giving you real cause for concern, you have to do whatever you think is the best for your pooch. Sometimes you have to make a snap decision to protect your dog and most owners of small dogs probably pick them up from time to time to avoid potential danger.

WHY ON EARTH IS MY DOG DOING THAT?

Sometimes our little furries do things that seem strange or even disgusting to us humans. Even the cleanest, sweetest-smelling diva dog can behave in a way that makes us blush or feel queasy. Don't worry – it's probably normal.

Bum-sniffing, for example, would not be my preferred method of saying hello, but dogs sniff each other's private bits in order to exchange information. There's no need to try to stop them doing this, they're just being dogs, although I think I'll stick to air-kissing and shaking hands myself.

It's more embarrassing when your furry sniffs your human friends in inappropriate places. This is particularly noticeable with dogs whose heads are conveniently crotch-height, but put a little one on

a lap and they may well try to have a good sniff. Again, they're just collecting information. Don't tell them off, just distract them to spare your blushes.

We've all seen dogs getting over-friendly with cushions, toys, other dogs or people's legs. This is either funny or mortifying – depending on who's watching. Surprisingly, mounting isn't a purely sexual behaviour; neutered males and females sometimes do it, too. It can be a way of showing dominance. There isn't really anything wrong with them doing this so you can just ignore it, but we humans do find it embarrassing, so distract them with a toy if you'd prefer them to stop. If the problem is persistent, you may want to consider consulting a behaviourist or trainer.

Another thing you probably don't want them doing in front of guests is 'scooting', or rubbing their bottom along the floor – like Roley opposite! This is quite funny to watch, but could be a symptom of worms or blocked anal glands; so if they're doing it a lot, a trip to the vet is probably best.

Humans have a natural aversion to horrible smells, but our delightful furry friends seem to love them. Given half a chance, they will roll in fox poo (which smells unbelievably revolting, believe me) or on dead rabbits or anything else they come across that you wouldn't go anywhere near. They do this because their inner-wolf is telling them to conceal their doggy scent with a camouflage of smells. Wolves do this so they can sneak up more easily on their prey. Our pampered pooches sometimes forget that they've come a long way since they had to catch their own dinner, which is why they roll in disgusting stuff. Luckily, you have a bathroom full of fragrant doggy products to remedy the problem when you get home.

HOW DO I KNOW
IF MY DOG IS UNWELL?

A regular once-over (see page 102) to check that everything is as it should be will help you identify any potential health problems.

In addition, your pooch should go to the vet's once a year for their booster jabs, which protect them against potentially fatal diseases such as distemper and canine parvovirus. Your vet will also check them over for any other problems.

Apart from that, you need to observe your dog closely for any signs of illness. When dogs don't feel very well, they generally make it fairly clear. They are experts at looking sorry for themselves and as you get to know your dog, you will soon learn to read the signs. A poorly pooch may become lethargic, restless, find it difficult to settle, appear to hunch their shoulders or lose their appetite. Look out for limping, stiffness, yelping at certain movements and a decline in coat quality.

Make sure you have your vet's emergency contact details handy and, as I've said before, I strongly recommend taking out pet insurance. Money is the last thing you want to worry about if you have to call the vet out in the middle of the night.

Dogs are also vulnerable to internal and external parasites, which are horrible to think about but, thankfully, fairly easy to avoid. Fleas and worms can lead to serious health problems if left unchecked, so it's best to follow a regular routine of preventative treatment. Your vet will advise on the best treatment for your pooch and how often you should administer it. Parasite treatments are not

SOME SIGNS TO WATCH OUT FOR

- ♥ Limping or stiff movements
- ♥ Coughing or wheezing
- ♥ Weight gain or loss
- ♥ Sensitivity when touched
- ♥ Runny poo
- ♥ Blood in poo or wee
- ♥ Vomiting or diarrhoea
- ♥ Constipation
- ♥ Frequent head shaking
- ♥ Unusual quietness
- ♥ Increased hunger or thirst
- ♥ Loss of appetite
- ♥ A hunched appearance
- ♥ Hair loss
- ♥ Weepy eyes or discharge from nose
- ♥ Dull coat
- ♥ Scratching
- ♥ Smelly ears

usually covered by pet insurance policies, so factor this cost into your dog-care budget. Remember, roundworms can be passed on to humans so it's important for both of you to get it sorted out properly.

AS YOUR DOG GETS OLDER

Just like us, dogs begin to slow down a bit as they hit middle age. Their hearing and eyesight may not be so good and they can become stiff in the joints and often go grey around the muzzle. Small pooches generally live longer than large dogs, so they stay young for longer. Lola is now seven, but she's still full of youthful vigour and doesn't seem anywhere near ready for retirement.

Still, old age comes to us all and you'll need to make adjustments to give your senior the very best care in their autumn years. It's an idea to increase the frequency of visits to the vet from once to twice a year and you may consider changing your dog's diet to a special senior formula. As dogs get stiffer and less agile, they probably won't want to go on strenuous walks and they'll certainly appreciate a super-comfy bed to sleep on. Older dogs may find it difficult to jump up on to their comfort spots so you might want to invest in a set of mini-stairs to help them get on the sofa. An older dog may lose their enthusiasm for the social whirl and may prefer to put their feet up as much as possible. If your little one's lived life in the fast lane, it may be time to slow down the pace a notch.

Use your grooming sessions to look out for signs of ageing that might need attention. Teeth are a particular problem in the older dog, and loose or decaying teeth can make it difficult for them to eat. In some cases, you'll need to have the teeth cleaned or removed by the vet. It's especially important at this time of life to look out for any growths,

lumps or warts on your dog's skin. Be gentle when grooming a senior because their skin becomes thinner and less supple, just as ours does as we age. A dog's senior years are not all about worry and illness. This is a very special time because you know each other so well and your older dog will be much calmer and less naughty than they perhaps were when they were younger. Give your super senior as much time as you can. They might not be so playful any more, but you will still get a great deal of pleasure out of each other's company.

TIME TO SAY GOODBYE

Very sadly, the day will come along when you have to say goodbye to your beloved friend. I haven't had to go through this experience yet and I honestly believe it's going to be one of the hardest days of my life. It's not something I really want to think about, but I know I have to face the prospect like a mature adult. When the time comes, I think it's important to have friends and family around you who truly understand your loss. Surround yourself with all your doggy friends who really respect the connection you had with your little diva dog. Don't be afraid to talk about your feelings, even if it makes you cry.

Since the day Lola came into my life I've done everything possible to show how much I appreciate her and to try to give her the best possible doggy existence I can. When the time finally comes to say goodbye, I think it's important to celebrate your pooch's life. I know some people make a scrapbook or have a box of mementoes to help them cherish the memory of their little friend. Pet funerals and cremations are possible these days – but that really is something I'm going to put off thinking about for now. In the meantime, I'm going to make the most of every single minute we have left together.

DOGGY DINING

Even diva dogs wolf down their food sometimes and they don't always have the best table manners. That's no excuse for cutting corners when it comes to a healthy, nutritious diet for your little star.

WAITER! MAY I SEE
THE MENU?

Because of my non-stop, hectic diva lifestyle, I don't always have the healthiest diet myself. It's hard to eat a balanced diet when you're constantly racing from one place to the next.

I'm always grabbing something on the run and I actually take much more care with my dogs' diet than my own.

My little furbabies have a breakfast of scrambled eggs with red pepper, which I cook myself, and they have a meal of high-quality dry food in the evening. They do have treats, but I'd never give them anything that was high in salt, fat or sugar. A lot of processed food for humans is full of these things so it's never a good idea to treat them with human snacks – no matter how longingly they stare at you with those cute eyes.

People often use food as a way of saying 'I love you', but if you're giving your dog unhealthy food, that's not really love – it's just irresponsible.

Diva dogs have a reputation for being pernickety eaters, but fussy dogs are generally made, not born. Let's be honest, our pampered pooches are very good at manipulating us. If they refuse to eat what's in their bowl, they can get us to hand-feed them delicious treats and give them extra attention. It's hard to resist that melting expression, but you don't really want your little treasure to be in charge of the menu.

Apart from anything else, a healthy, balanced diet is essential to keep your little star looking fabulous. A good diet will improve skin and coat quality no end and is just as important as fancy shampoos. There is definitely some truth in the saying 'you are what you eat', so remember this every time you reach for your little one's food. A properly fed dog will look stunning and feel wonderful.

WHAT DO **DOGS EAT?**

Our doggies' wild ancestors couldn't afford to be picky about food and most dogs will eat a wide range of foodstuffs, whether or not it's actually any good for them.

Dogs will eat most of the things we do, but that doesn't mean it's suitable to share your meals with them. Avoid giving them fatty, sugary or spicy food. Dogs are not exclusively meat eaters so a healthy doggy diet should include protein, fat, carbohydrates, vitamins, minerals and fibre.

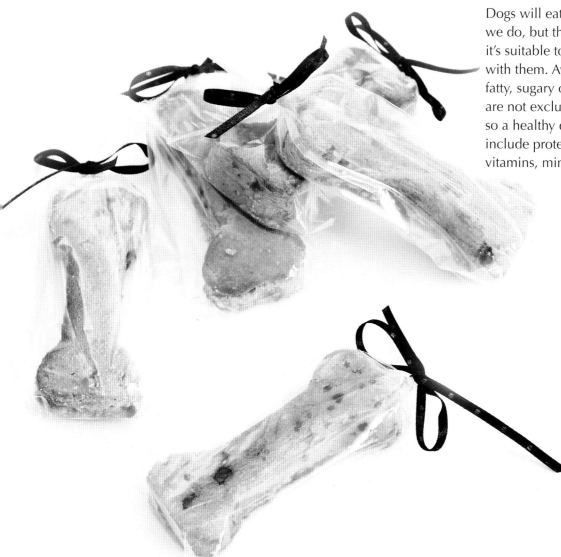

TYPE OF DOG FOOD

I find that the cheapest is rarely the best, and this is just as true of dog food as it is of shoes or face cream. Your best friend's health is more important than anything, so it's worth investing in a premium dog food. These are carefully balanced to make sure dogs get all the nutrients they need. You wouldn't be very healthy if you lived on sweets and junk food forever, and it's exactly the same for your pooch. If you have a little, tiny dog, they don't eat very much, so you can afford to splash out.

Never feed cat food to your dog because it has a much higher meat content than dog food – and that's too much protein for a woofer (besides, it smells really horrible and their deposits will be very yucky).

DRY OR WET?

Dogs can be fed on wet tinned or dry food, depending on their preference. A complete dry food is particularly good for dogs because having something to crunch removes some of the plaque and tartar from their teeth and helps avoid dental problems. Some dry food is too big for little dogs to deal with, so opt for small dog varieties that your mini-love will be able to get their teeth around. Lots of dogs seem to like a little wet food, too – so if poochie is turning up their nose at dry biscuits, just mix in a little tinned food or moisten the biscuits with a drop of water.

RAW-FOOD DIETS

Some people believe that it's wrong to feed dogs any food that is processed or even cooked. Fans of raw-food diets argue that it is more natural. Dogs on this diet are fed on raw meat, bones and uncooked vegetables. This approach causes a lot of arguments among doggy people and there are strong feelings on both sides. If you think your pooch would be better eating like back

in the old days when they were still living in the wild, make sure you discuss it with your vet first.

SPECIAL DIETS

These days, there are all sorts of products for dogs with different needs. Life-stage foods are available for puppies, adults and senior dogs and you can get food that is specially designed for different breeds. There are also veterinary diets available, which your vet might recommend for particular conditions such as allergies or skin problems.

TREATS

The diva dog should have perfect table manners and not humiliate themselves by begging from the table. No matter how tempting, never feed your dog titbits from the table.

There are nutritious treats available, but even these can pile on the calories if given too generously. Remember to count any treats as part of your dog's daily diet. For a healthy alternative, try a little bit of carrot, celery or pepper – some dogs love munching on something crunchy.

Treats don't always have to be edible. An extra bit of love and attention can be just as much of a reward.

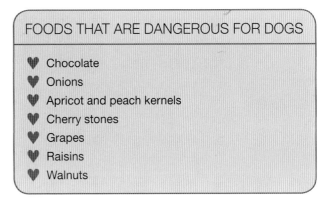

FOODS THAT ARE DANGEROUS FOR DOGS

- ♥ Chocolate
- ♥ Onions
- ♥ Apricot and peach kernels
- ♥ Cherry stones
- ♥ Grapes
- ♥ Raisins
- ♥ Walnuts

HOW MUCH SHOULD
I FEED MY DOG?

The amount of food a dog needs depends on their size, age, breed and level of activity.

Small dogs have a high metabolism, so they burn off calories quickly, especially when they are puppies. But each dog is different so keep an eye on them and adjust the quantity of food if they lose or put on weight.

Make sure you read the instructions carefully and measure out the food properly (don't just guess!). Remember, if you change brands you may have to adjust the quantity.

IS YOUR POOCH TOO PLUMP?

Sadly, far too many dogs are overweight these days, which can lead to heart disease, bone and joint problems and even diabetes. We all want to show our furbabies how much we love them, but cupboard love can be very harmful. Find out what your dog's ideal weight should be and weigh them from time to time.

If you can't feel their ribs when pressing lightly, your pooch is probably overweight and you may need to consider putting them on a calorie-controlled diet. Many vet's surgeries run weight-control clinics where you can get help and advice. Just as with our own waistlines, it's much easier to stop your pooch getting tubby in the first place than it is to get the extra weight off. Once again, prevention is better than cure.

FOOD AND
WATER BOWLS

A heavy ceramic or stainless steel bowl with a non-slip rubber bottom is best. There are some very cute bowls available, even jewel-encrusted ones.

Make sure the bowls are not too high if your pooch is tiny and has short legs.

If you have a dog with long, floppy ears, such as a spaniel, you may find that they get food on their ears when they're eating. You can buy special bowls to prevent this, which have a narrow top and stand high off the floor. Another popular option is a little hat that looks like a shower cap and allows them to munch away without their ears flopping into their dinner – much more hygienic!

Elevated feeding stations are great if you have a large-breed dog because it means they can eat at a comfortable height without having to bend their necks right to the floor.

Make sure there is always fresh water available for your furry friend, and keep their bowls and feeding area nice and clean. No one wants to eat off a dirty dinner plate – especially a little diva.

GROOMING &
PAMPERING

Great hair takes time, care and an excellent groomer. A regular pamper regime keeps your pooch looking fabulous and gives you the chance to make sure your little one is healthy as well as beautiful.

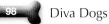

DIVAS DON'T DO
BAD HAIR DAYS

As you might expect, I put a fair bit of effort into my own hair – or at least my hairdresser does. I see him once a week and he works wonders with my tresses.

I can't imagine how I'd manage my naturally curly mane without him. Despite my commitment to my own hair-care regime, doggy hairdressing didn't even cross my mind when Lola first came to live with me. To be honest, I didn't even know what a dog groomer was. Puppy coats change quickly and I was surprised when Lola's hair became really long in no time at all. Thinking back to her original look, she didn't look very pretty. It was clearly time for me to seek out the services of a professional groomer.

Our first trip to a groomer was not entirely successful. In fact, I'd go as far as to say it was a total disaster. I had handed over my little girl expecting her to be returned to me looking good enough to win Crufts. But that's not what happened at all. I was horrified when the groomer handed my Lola back. She was shaky and scared and resembled a very closely shorn sheep. Alarm bells rang and I immediately started searching for another groomer. I felt so awful about giving my little one to a woman who had clearly terrified her. It took ages for her fur to grow back and she wore quite a few t-shirts for several months.

The search was on for someone I could trust completely to be Lola's personal groomer and it wasn't until I decided to open my own grooming parlour that I finally found a groomer who really, really understands dogs.

I want all the pooches who come to my parlour to feel totally comfortable and to see the experience as an enjoyable pamper time rather than their worst nightmare. Together with my staff, I worked on packages that each dog would love. Lola sees her groomer once a week (just like me!). She has her hair brushed, trimmed and washed with high-quality shampoo that's formulated for her coat type. It's a moisturising shampoo that helps keep her locks soft and shiny and she has a conditioning treatment, like us humans, which keeps dull and lifeless locks at bay. She also has her nails done. They are filed and buffed to perfection – paw-di-cures are definitely a diva dog must. Her ears are plucked and cleaned and she gets a little massage.

Lola loves her pamper sessions and always comes sashaying out of the salon looking like a star.

Now, I know that opening a grooming parlour for your furry one isn't practical for most people. You can do a lot of grooming yourself at home; however you never really get the same finish as you would with a professional. I do understand that it's not practical or affordable for everyone to go to the groomer's every week. Even so, I do recommend professional grooming every six to eight weeks for coated breeds. This will keep them hot to trot and make life easier for you. Even if you treat your pooch to regular professional grooming, you'll still need to be prepared to do some work yourself. Our little ones deserve the best so make sure you give it to them.

WHY GOOD GROOMING IS ESSENTIAL

Now, with any diva dog appearance is very important. You owe it to your pooch to make sure they don't look like they've been dragged through a hedge backwards. Naturally, you'll want your dog to be clean, presentable and looking fabulous. But grooming is about much more than fur-deep beauty. Brushing spreads natural oils around the coat, making it all glossy and gorgeous. Regular grooming sessions are also a chance to spend some special time together as well as to check for any health problems.

Tangled and matted coats not only look dreadful, they can lead to itchy, sore skin and cause infections. It's very sad when pups come to us who have never had a brush or bath. It often means that all their lovely fur has to be cut very short because it has become so matted that it would be too painful to brush. Once it's got this bad, it's very difficult to deal with. Fortunately, it's easy enough to avoid this happening if you get into a regular grooming routine.

PAMPERING **YOUR PUPPY**

While your puppy is still too young to go out to the park, they are unlikely to get really dirty, but this is the perfect time to get them started on a cleaning and grooming routine.

Start with just a few minutes at a time and make it a fun experience for both of you.

Get your puppy used to the brushes and combs they are going to have to deal with for the rest of their lives. Even if they don't actually need a brush, put them on a table and gently brush them while giving them treats and praise. It's also a very good idea to try using a hairdryer on a very low setting to prepare them for when their coats are fully grown and they really do need a good groom.

If you get a puppy who is going to need professional grooming, make an appointment for them as soon as they are fully vaccinated. There's no need to have the full works on your first visit; this is an opportunity for your little one to meet the groomer and get used to all the strange equipment and noises. A good grooming salon will take your dog's first visit slowly and book extra time to get them comfortable and relaxed. After all, the whole experience is completely unfamiliar and you want to make it as pleasant as possible.

THE WEEKLY **ONCE-OVER**

Your grooming regime will depend on breed and coat type. Many dogs need to be brushed several times a week, or even daily.

Whatever type of dog you have, put aside at least 15 minutes a week to give them a really thorough going over to check everything is as it should be.

If you've got a small pooch, it's easier to do this on a table. Place them on a non-slip surface (a towel will do) and run your hands over their body to check for lumps, bumps or scratches. Check their coat for fleas and ticks and look out for bits of twig or leaf that can easily get caught in long coats. If you have a long-coated breed, you should also check the hair round the bum – I don't want to be indelicate, but doo-doo can get stuck in the fur in that area. Make sure the eyes, ears and teeth are clean and that there is nothing stuck in their paw pads or between their toes. Grass seeds can be particularly painful.

Ears – Clean the inside of the ear with some moistened cotton wool; use a different piece for each ear to prevent cross-infection. You may also use a few drops of ear-cleaning solution. Don't push anything into the ear canal as this could cause damage. Make sure the hair around the ears is also clean. Watch out for redness or a bad smell; this could be a sign of ear mites. Long-haired dogs sometimes need to have their ear hair plucked or trimmed – this is best done by a professional.

Eyes – Gently and carefully clean the area around the eyes with a damp cloth or cottonwool ball. Dust can cause irritation or infection so keep a look-out for any discharge or redness. Some dogs produce quite a lot of tears, which can stain the fur. This is particularly visible on white dogs. Sometimes this can be caused by a medical condition, so it's worth checking with your vet. I've been told by quite a few clients that there are many ways of reducing tear staining, such as only giving your pooch filtered water, feeding them on light-coloured foods or putting ice cubes in their water. I haven't tried any of these methods myself so I can't say how well they work – but they could be worth a go.

Teeth – Teeth should be cleaned at least once a week to prevent the build-up of tartar. Not only will this help to reduce pongy breath, it will also keep teeth and gums healthy. You can buy special doggy toothpaste (never be tempted to use human toothpaste on a dog) and tiny toothbrushes. Not all dogs like to be poked about in the mouth, so it's a good idea to get them used to this when they are puppies. Small dogs suffer more from dental problems than bigger dogs, so it's vital to keep their little gnashers in good condition. Chew toys, Nylabones and crunchy food will also help keep their teeth gleaming white.

Feet and nails – Check between the toes to make sure nothing is stuck there. Long-haired dogs may also need to have the hair around the feet trimmed to keep them neat. Check the nails to make sure they are not too long. Overgrown nails can get caught in things (your favourite outfit, for example) which could be painful and lead to the nail being broken or even pulled out. If left too long, the nails can curl up and grow into the paw – you can imagine how painful that is. Big dogs often wear down their nails naturally when they're out and about, but many tiny dogs are so light that they don't put enough pressure on their nails when they walk to file them down.

If you're going to cut the nails yourself, buy special doggy nail clippers. It's not particularly easy to do this and not all dogs are very keen on the experience. Get your puppy used to having their feet and toes played with as early as possible and start off by clipping just the very tip of the nail. It's important to avoid cutting the quick – which is inside the nail and will bleed if cut. If your dog has white claws, it's fairly easy to see where the quick finishes because it's pink. For dogs with black nails, it's impossible to be sure exactly where the quick finishes. If you're not confident enough to have a go, get a professional groomer to do it.

BATH **TIME**

People often ask me how often they should bath their furbabies.
The answer depends on your tolerance for smelly dogs.

Mine have a bath once a week, but this isn't necessary for all dogs. Short-coated breeds may not need a bath as often, but remember they can still smell. Coated breeds will need more frequent baths to keep them looking and smelling lovely. It's best to invest in a decent quality shampoo that will not dry out your dog's coat or leave them itching. Small dogs can be given a bath in the sink, but you'll need to use the bathtub for larger furry friends. Use a non-slip mat so they don't slide about.

Always brush your baby before their bath and never use human shampoo. Dog's skin has a different pH to human skin and our shampoo can irritate them. If you do get stuck, the safest thing would be to use baby shampoo – but do try and stick to doggy cleanser. It's definitely worth stocking up on some good-quality shampoo – after all, you wouldn't use any old cheap shampoo on your own hair, would you? Spending a bit more is worthwhile because quality products last longer than cheaper varieties as they are more concentrated.

Be careful not to get shampoo in your pooch's eyes or ears, unless you have a tearless shampoo, otherwise it can sting. I make sure all my furkids and our clients are washed in tearless puppy shampoo around their faces and bottoms and normal shampoo on their bodies. Always make sure you rinse them off thoroughly as leaving in shampoo or conditioner is not good for them. Rinse until the water runs clear.

Short-coated dogs can be towel-dried, but you'll also need a hairdryer on a low or medium setting for many coated breeds. It can take a long time to get a long-coated dog properly dry, so this may be something you'd prefer to get a professional to do.

COAT **TYPES**

Talk to your breeder or groomer about how best to look after different coat types. They are the experts, after all.

Your breeder or groomer will be able to advise on which hairstyles work best on which breeds. I really wouldn't recommend giving your pooch anything more than the tiniest trim yourself (imagine how awful we would look if we cut our own hair), so if you've got a dog that needs trimming or clipping, go to a professional.

These are the most common coat types, with my tips on essential care:

Short and smooth coats (dachshunds, pugs, bulldogs) – These coats are the easiest to look after and need little more than a weekly brush to remove dirt, dead skin and hair. These coats can shed quite heavily all year round, so a regular brush will reduce the amount of vacuuming you have to do. The ideal tool for this is a soft-bristled brush or a hound mitt – which is a glove with a brush on one side and a smooth surface on the other side for polishing. Rubber brushes are also great as they stimulate the hair and have an exfoliating effect.

Long and silky coats (shih-tzus, Yorkies, Maltese) – These beautiful, flowing coats can tangle easily and need daily brushing. The best tool for this is a pin brush, or the slicker brush variation, or a comb. If the coat is already matted, it's best to get professional help. These coats will also need regular

trimming around the ears and feet. Left to grow to their natural length, long, silky coats can be very hard to look after and keep clean, so many owners prefer to have a shorter look.

Lola's hair, for instance, is a look that I created for her years ago. She has her own style, called the Lola cut. She's cut fairly short on the body with flared legs at the bottom. This works very well for her as she wears clothes and it eliminates that hairy chest syndrome, which can make her look like a medallion man. The flared legs and feet work fantastically as they flow when she walks, a little bit like a shire horse. This look is good on most long silky coats.

Wiry coats (schnauzers and most types of terrier) – Wire-coated dogs don't in fact need a huge amount of maintenance, but they do shed, especially in spring and autumn. Weekly brushing will remove dead hair but the top coat needs to be hand-stripped at least three times a year. Hair grows at different rates, depending on the dog, so you should get your groomer's advice on how often is best for you. This process will keep the texture to the coat. Clipping, on the other hand, will change the texture, making it softer and finer. Regular trips to a professional groomer will help keep your wiry friend looking spruce and dapper.

Curly coats (poodles, bichons frisés) – These coats look fabulous, but really do need some attention. They don't shed, but it's essential that the coat isn't left to get tangled or matted and they should be bathed around once a month. The coat can take a long time to dry. You will need a pin brush or slicker for daily brushing. It's best to get curly-coated dogs professionally groomed every six to eight weeks. They will need to be trimmed or clipped. This coat is easy to mould because the thick curls hold their shape. Many cuts are possible – my personal favourite has to be the little pompoms that they can have, but creative hairstyling is best left to a professional.

Thick and bushy coats (Pomeranians, huskies) – These coats are high-maintenance and need daily brushing and combing. Breeds with this type of fur have a double coat. The undercoat is the dog's insulation system and it's important that you comb to the skin to prevent the undercoat from matting. Dogs with this type of coat can develop serious skin conditions if they are not correctly groomed, so it helps to have a professional's assistance. As with other coated breeds, a trip to the groomer's every six to eight weeks is recommended.

WHAT TO EXPECT FROM YOUR GROOMER

I think it's really important to get your dog acquainted with a reputable groomer as soon as possible. The best way to find a good groomer is to speak to other dog owners or ask your breeder. No groomer deserves your money unless they really love and respect dogs. Expect your groomer to be patient and willing to answer all your questions, and, above all, to have that magic doggy touch that is so important for putting our pooches at ease. It's probably best for you not to stay with your pooch

while they're being pampered. You'll just fuss and your doggy won't know who they're supposed to be responding to. Just like children, poochies can play up more if they know mum and dad are around. I always tell my clients that their dog will let them know if they are happy. You'll be able to see from their reaction when they leave the parlour. Having said that, my best friend brings her Yorkie to our parlour every four weeks. Of course, the little pooch has never been mistreated; she knows us all so well and has a brilliant time with us. All the same, as soon as her mum collects her she starts to shake. Now, this could just be excitement, so do try to read your dog's signs – we don't want you making any rash decisions.

Don't be afraid to ask your groomer lots of questions. How long have they been grooming? Have they groomed your type of dog before? What do they do if a dog is nervous? Do they have references from people you could contact before you go? A groomer who really cares should understand that this is the customer's baby and they should be prepared for questions. We wouldn't just leave our human child with a sitter without vetting them first, would we?

DIVA DOGS ESSENTIAL GROOMING KIT

- ♥ Hound mitt
- ♥ Slicker brush
- ♥ Comb
- ♥ Pin brush
- ♥ Nail clippers
- ♥ Scissors
- ♥ Clippers
- ♥ Ear/eye wipes
- ♥ Shampoo

LUXURY EXTRAS FOR THE TRUE DIVA

If you want to go that extra mile for your little one,
you can ask your groomer for special treatments.
Some favourites with my clients are:

- ♥ Massages
- ♥ Nail painting
- ♥ Coat colouring
- ♥ Facials
- ♥ Sparkle gloss shine
- ♥ Creative cuts such as Mohicans

It takes a lot of effort to look this good

ALL THE COLOURS OF THE RAINBOW

Just like us, dogs can diva it up with flamboyant hair colours. Red, pink, blue, yellow – you name it, you can get it.

While it can be cute to have a pink fluffy fur ball, you must only use dog-friendly coat dye from a specialist supplier. Never, ever use human hair dye on a dog – it could be extremely dangerous. I strongly recommend that colour changes should only ever be carried out by a professional.

It is also important that you do not dye your dog's coat if they are shy or introverted, as a brightly coloured dog will attract lots of attention. Pooches with sensitive skin or allergies are not ideal models for this dramatic look either – we wouldn't want you to have to deal with any bad reactions.

LET'S GO
WALKIES

7

These paws were made for walking and even the most sophisticated pooch looks forward to a walk in the park. Of course, style and exercise are not incompatible so put your designer wellies on and get your diva some gorgeous gear for the great outdoors.

GIVING YOUR DIVA
THE RUN AROUND

The daily dog walk is one of my favourite times of the day because it's a chance for me to spend some special time with my little furries.

Lola and her siblings get taken out for about an hour a day and this is when they really get to express their dogginess. It's amazing how much pleasure they get out of the simplest things – sniffing a blade of grass or weeing on a dandelion. It gives me such a buzz to see them enjoying themselves so much.

If you have a very small dog and a reasonably sized garden, you might think you don't need to take them out for a walk. We've all seen a Chihuahua or a Yorkie run themselves dizzy in the smallest of spaces. It's true that petite pooches don't need acres of fields or a four-hour hike, but dogs like a change of scene just as much as we do and even the teeniest pooch enjoys getting out and about.

A regular exercise regime will burn off all that doggy energy and make your dog much more chilled-out for the rest of the day. A good run off their sparkly lead helps to keep dogs fit and slim and the exercise will do you good too. So pull on your pink wellies and get walking!

From a dog's point of view, going for a walk is about much more than just getting some exercise. Even a small local park is one big amusement centre full of thrills and surprises. Dogs love to sniff, play, chase, make friends and catch up with the gossip – every lamppost is covered with juicy information about who's in the neighbourhood. It's like catching up on all the social goings-on, similar to us humans having a night out with friends.

Most people have one particular spot where they usually take their furry friends for a walk and you're likely to make friends with other regular walkers, which will increase your dog's social circle – and possibly yours, too. Just because you're going to the same place every day doesn't mean the walk has to be boring. I often vary my route so the walk doesn't become too humdrum.

It's also really lovely to use your walks as a chance to play together. Our pooches are highly in tune with us, so we should return the favour by paying our best friends some attention. It makes me feel sad when I'm out with my dogs and I see people who are too busy on their mobile phones or jogging or cycling to notice what their canine companions are up to. Dogs need mental as well as physical stimulation, so get yourself a tennis ball or frisbee and play games or do tricks while you're out. This is your time together, so make the most of it.

When you get the chance, go somewhere special for a walk. Most dogs love running on the beach or exploring the countryside. Wherever you live, there are probably lots of places nearby that are ideal for doggy fun – just make sure that dogs are allowed before you set out (not everywhere is as doggy-friendly as we'd like it to be).

Above all, your walks should be enjoyable for both of you. Fifi Trixibelle might get wet, might get muddy, might even roll in something you don't even want to think about – but you can worry about all that when you get home. While you're out, let your little star be a dog.

HOW MUCH EXERCISE DOES MY DOG NEED?

The amount of exercise a dog needs varies considerably and depends on the dog's size, breed, age and temperament. If you have a pedigree dog, ask the breeder and other owners of the breed for advice about exercise needs. Most small dogs need more exercise than many people realise. An hour a day is a good walk for most small breeds (you could go for one long walk or two short ones), with longer trips out from time to time. A shorter walk will satisfy some of the short-nosed breeds such as pugs, Pekingese and bulldogs.

Some dogs want to go out whatever the weather, but others would rather stay warm and dry. If your furry walking companion isn't impressed by miserable weather, you don't have to drag them out in hail, sleet and snow. When the weather is awful, abandon the walk for the day, but make an extra effort to play indoors so they still get some exercise. If you have one of those outdoorsy dogs, you'll just have to put on your wellies and waterproofs. Older dogs may need less exercise, but some of them

are still going strong long after they've collected their pensions, so listen to your dog – if they're still enjoying their walks, stick with it, but cut back if they seem overtired or uncomfortable.

If your furry friend is putting on weight or becoming difficult or destructive in the house, it may be because they're not getting enough exercise.

GET KITTED OUT **IN STYLE**

My dogs are almost always dressed to impress when they go out.

Yes, it's true, they're usually wearing matching harnesses – a frilly number for the girls, carefully co-ordinated with something a bit more butch for my little boy, Larry. If it's a bit chilly I make sure that they have a cute fleece or jumper or maybe a coat. But I'd never put fashion before practicality. All my dogs wear a collar when they're out, but I attach their leads to a harness, which is generally better for small dogs. They have delicate little necks and a lead attached to a collar could cause too much strain. As I have four dogs, I also use a coupler, which attaches to the end of the lead and allows you to walk two dogs on one lead. This saves a lot of hassle, especially if you have lively little dogs who dance about and twist their leads around like a maypole.

Safety is the most important thing to consider when buying collars, leads, harnesses, outdoor coats and accessories. The equipment you need will depend on size and breed. Luckily, it's easy to be safe, secure and stylish with today's doggy fashion ranges. You can choose to go with glitzy, frilly and fabulous, but comfort and safety are never optional extras.

Talking of safety, dogs should always wear an ID tag with your contact details. This is a legal requirement and also means that if your little darling should run off on a walk or escape from your home, you have a very good chance of being reunited. It's still worth getting a microchip even if your pooch never leaves home without ID – lost dogs can lose their collars.

COLLARS AND LEADS

Dog collars come in a variety of widths: generally, the bigger the dog, the wider the collar you'll need. Bear in mind that a thick sparkly collar with rows and rows of diamante isn't necessarily the best choice for a small dog with a tiny neck – we don't want them to feel like they're wearing a neck brace. Make sure the collar is tight enough so that your dog can't pull their head out of it but loose enough for comfort – you should be able to fit two fingers under the collar.

If you have a puppy, it's a good idea to get them used to wearing a collar as soon as possible. Not all pet shops sell collars small enough for petite pooches, especially tiny breed puppies, so you might have to shop around for something that is safe and fits properly (not to mention stylish). Whatever you do, don't buy a cat collar. Don't get me wrong, some of them are really cute, but they are designed with a quick-release feature just in case puss gets stuck somewhere. The last thing you want is a collar that pops open easily, so cat collars are definitely not safe for dogs.

Some people still use choke chains on their dogs. This is a metal chain which tightens round the dog's neck if they pull on the lead. I'm really not a fan of these. They are a horrible idea and can be dangerous – particularly for dainty dogs. I would never recommend a choke chain for any dog, unless you are a professional handler using it for specialised training work. A diva dog should never need a choke chain – apart from anything else, they're so ugly.

Extendable leads are very useful if you're walking somewhere poochie can't go off lead and you want to give them more freedom than they'd get on a normal lead. These leads extend up to between five and 15 metres, but they reduce the control you have over your dog, so you need to be very careful if you are walking near a road. If something exciting happens on the other side of the road, your dog could rush out in front of a car before you have chance to react. Extendable leads have a lock button so you can prevent this from happening, but it's probably safer to use a normal lead when walking your dog in busy places.

HARNESSES

Step-in harnesses are great for dogs who are not so easy to get into their walking gear and they're also brilliant if your pooch is wearing a little winter coat as the harness can go over the outfit.

Soft harnesses are perfect for all dogs and especially great for puppies because they are made of material that is soft and easily washed.

Thick, leather harnesses give you control with stronger, larger diva dogs, such as bulldogs. Leather harnesses are available for small dogs, too. You can get soft, buttery-textured ones that

mould with your little one as you use them, a bit like a great pair of Jimmy Choos. Bear in mind that if you spend a lot of money on a fabulously flashy harness, you won't want to be using it if you're trekking in the forest or skinny-dipping in the sea – treat it as if it were a pair of designer Louboutins.

A coat/dress harness is for special occasions when a diva dog feels the need to impress. This is a very pretty harness which looks like a coat, dress or outerwear but has a little loop at the back where you can attach a lead. This means your little love can be perfectly safe without compromising on style.

KEEPING WARM **AND DRY**

If your pooch is a true prince or princess, they probably won't entertain puddles. But even a diva dog needs to go out, so a weather-proof coat is essential.

Horse rug-style waterproof coats are great for most dogs. They sit on the dog's back, leaving all four legs to move freely. They usually do up with one fastening around the neck and another around the tummy. You could also opt for a waterproof, bodywarmer-style coat, which covers the body and doesn't enclose the legs.

Some waterproof coats have front leg holes with little sleeves, just like a coat we would wear. It can sometimes take a while for your little one to get used to this, but these are one of the most popular types of outdoor doggy clothing. Just make sure the coat fits properly and doesn't restrict movement. If your pooch can't move around easily, they're in the wrong outerwear – get straight back to the shops and start again!

All-in-one waterproofs are a fantastic invention for dogs that love the wet outdoors. They cover all four legs, just like a child's babygrow, except they have an opening for the toilet business and a hole for their waggy tails. These all-in-ones are perfect if you want to keep your furkid

dry and clean. They are also brilliant in the snow because they help stop all those snowballs that our poor pooches end up bringing home (they're a nightmare to defrost!). Remember, not all dogs will tolerate wearing an all-in-one, so listen to your pooch – they will let you know if snow-proof gear is for them or not.

FOOTWEAR

You can purchase an array of doggy footwear for all types of weather, from summer sandals to waterproof wellie boots. To be honest, my Lola has never got on with them. I tried boots once, but she walked as if she was wearing a pair of flippers so we didn't try them again. Still, I'm not saying your diva can't rock the latest set of poochie pumps.

THE WELL-MANNERED
WALKING
COMPANION

One of the most important things to teach your dog is to come back to you when they're off the lead.

This is called recall and it could not only save you the embarrassment of running round the park shouting, it could also save your dog's life – although, I have to admit, it can be amusing when your other half is trying hard to keep up his macho image while calling out 'Tootsie Tinkerbell'. Your walks will also be much less stressful for both of you if you teach your pooch to walk nicely on the lead, without constantly pulling and tugging.

Dogs love charging around off the lead, but the true diva dog is polite in public and doesn't bark at children, chase cyclists or jump up at joggers. Early socialisation and a bit of time invested in basic training will make your walks a pleasant experience.

SCOOP THE POOP!

In most places, it's a legal requirement to clean up dog poop and you could be fined if you get caught leaving your dog's business in a public place.

Besides, any truly pampered pooch would be mortified if their poop was left lying around.
You always flush the toilet after you've been, don't you? So don't embarrass your dog by leaving their mess where someone might step in it.

Never leave home without a supply of poo bags. Blingy poo bags are available for the fashion-conscious dog owner.

OMG! YOUR DOG'S SOOO CUTE!!

DEALING WITH FANS

If you have an adorable dog, it's highly likely that you will attract a lot of attention when you're out together. People, especially children, will crowd round you, coo, aaah and ask if they can stroke your super-cute pooch. Some dogs love this sort of attention and will happily put their best paw forward to work a crowd. But for some dogs, particularly tiny ones, this experience can be very intimidating. Even the sweetest-natured dog can become timid or snappy in this situation. Never be afraid to politely ask people not to touch your dog if you feel it could cause distress.

ON THE PULL – HOW TO TEACH YOUR DOG TO WALK ON A LEAD

Start off by practising in the house or garden. Put on the lead and walk around, keeping the lead slack. If your dog pulls, stop still. Wait until they calm down and the lead is slack again. Be sure to give them lots of praise and a food treat. Once they get the hang of this, say 'heel' while they are walking at your side and give them a treat.

Keep practising until your dog is happy trotting alongside you at your pace without pulling on the lead. This is easy enough in the relatively relaxed atmosphere of your home, but it's much harder to keep this up when you're outside, where there are all sorts of distractions like cats, squirrels, birds, interesting smells and other dogs. Keep practising and use lots and lots of praise. Make sure your best chum knows you're pleased with them when they walk nicely on the lead.

COME **BACK!!!**

Now, I'm the first to admit that I'm no Cesar Millan – dog training is not one of my finest talents.

That doesn't mean I'm not prepared to give it a go, though, especially when it comes to teaching my little loves to come back to me. This is one way to teach recall that I found useful.

Start recall training in your home or garden where your dog will be safe and there are few distractions. As you both become more confident, you can continue training outdoors. Use a long training lead to start with so it's easier to grab your dog if they do decide to go for a sprint.

THE RECALL

Step 1: Put your dog on a lead and ask them to sit.

Step 2: Keeping the lead loose, walk backwards a few paces.

Step 3: Using a friendly voice, say your dog's name and call 'come'.

Step 4: When they come towards you, give them a tasty treat and lots of praise.

Step 5: Gradually increase the distance they have to go to get the treat.

PRACTICE MAKES PERFECT

Little and often is always best with dog training. Practise recall in different parts of the house and garden and at different times so your dog gets used to being alert to your call. Recall and reward several times during a walk. If you only do it right at the end, your dog will associate it with going home, and may decide it's more fun to stay out and play.

CELEBRATE SUCCESS

End each session on a success so it's a positive experience. Never express anger – coming back to you should be the best thing in the world, so tell them how clever they are every time they get it right.

TEEN REBEL

Many puppies go through a teenage rebellion phase at about 6–12 months. You may find that your perfect puppy who always comes back to you suddenly starts to be more and more disobedient, especially when off the lead in an exciting place. Keep your nerve and stick with the training programme. If they do run away from you, resist the temptation to chase after them. They will just think you're playing a game. Instead, run in the opposite direction – a dog's natural instinct will be to follow you.

MAKE IT FUN

Remember – if you want your best friend to come back to you, you need to be more exciting than anything else around. Don't be too embarrassed to wave your arms in the air and shout their name in a super-excited tone. We all know how our furry ones love that baby voice we do and it always gets their attention. It helps if you crouch down so you are at doggy level.

Never shout at your dog – racing around in the big wide world is much more appealing than returning to an angry person. Even if that angry person loves you more than life itself.

YOUR CARRIER
AWAITS

You'll want to have your diva with you as often as possible and that means when travelling. At those moments when walking is not an option, you'll need something suitably stylish to get your pooch from one social engagement to another.

GET CARRIED AWAY
IN STYLE

All dogs should have the opportunity to walk every day. Dogs that are constantly carried around don't get the chance to do natural doggy things like sniffing smells and saying hello to other dogs.

There are times, though, when a dog needs to be in a carrier for safety – in a car or on public transport, for example, or if you are in a very crowded place. I have a bit of a handbag habit myself, and don't dare admit how much money I've spent on them, but I'd never carry my dogs in an ordinary handbag, even if it was the latest Louis, Prada or Chanel. It's just not safe. They need to be in a carrier that is designed for dogs. You can get a plain old thing that will do the job from any pet shop, but, let's face it, diva dog owners like to indulge in sexy, sophisticated and stylish bags. I always shop around for something funky and fashionable. The dog's comfort, of course, comes first. Beyond that, go crazy and get the bag that you will enjoy carrying.

Don't forget that even small dogs can start to feel heavy if you have to carry them for a while. One tiny Yorkie won't put too much strain on your shoulder, but I wouldn't want to go too far with a larger diva dog in a handbag.

DIVA DOG TRAVEL ESSENTIALS

If you're going out for the day with your dog, don't leave home without these essentials:

- ♥ Portable water bowl
- ♥ Dog food
- ♥ Cosy blanket
- ♥ Poo bags

Strengthened fastenings
for extra safety – a good carrier should be designed to carry a dog weighing up to 10lb; flimsy fittings just won't do the job.

Top opening
for easy access, with mesh cover to let in air and light.

Side opening
with closable mesh cover allows your pooch to look out.

THE PERFECT CARRIER

A proper dog carrier should have a safety clip so that the dog can be secured inside. There needs to be enough room for the dog to move around and air vents so the dog can breathe properly. You can't just shove all your stuff in the bag with the dog. This would be like expecting your beloved pooch to travel in the luggage hold rather than first class. Fortunately, you can buy carriers which have a separate compartment to hold your lip gloss, mobile phone, perfume and all the other bits and pieces us girls love to carry around.

You will probably have seen strollers or buggies used to get dogs about. For most pooches, there's no need to have a set of wheels. But if you have a number of dogs or a dog with mobility problems for one reason or another, you may find a stroller useful. I remember having Lola in her first stroller and a lady who wanted to see my new baby nearly jumped out of her skin when she realised my baby was furry. Again, it should be something that's designed with dogs in mind. Human toddlers have different needs to canine babies – they don't run very fast, for a start. A buggy or stroller for a dog should be fully enclosed and secure so the dog can't escape. It should also have safety clips so that you don't end up trying to catch your pooch leaping from their chariot.

It's not really a bag to a dog – it's just a cosy, enclosed place where they feel snuggly safe.

TAKING YOUR POOCH
FOR A DRIVE

If your pooch is going to go on road trips, you'll need a safe, comfortable carrier or a dog car seat that can be secured firmly in your car.

Never leave a dog unrestrained on the passenger or back seat or carry them on your lap.

Apart from anything else, driving under the influence of a seriously cute pooch could get you into trouble with the police. The Highway Code states that you should make sure dogs are restrained in the car so they can't distract you while you're driving. A seatbelt harness, pet carrier, dog cage or dog guard are all practical ways of keeping you and your dog safe on the road.

You shouldn't leave your dog alone in a car, especially in warm weather. The inside of a car can get extremely hot on a sunny day and dogs don't sweat, so they find it much more difficult than us to cool down. Even with the windows down, dogs can die in minutes. Every year we read horrible stories about dogs dying in hot cars, it's so sad. Please make sure your little darling isn't one of them.

Enclosed carrier
Perfect for that
sense of security.

YOUR CARRIAGE AWAITS

There are a number of different carriers with quirky designs. Here are some of my favourites:

Enclosed pet carrier – This is similar to a ladies' gym bag, fully closed with openings at both ends or from the top (air vents as standard). They can be soft and mould like a normal handbag or they can be hard-sided, which can be used as a safety carrier.

Open pet carrier – Also similar to a ladies' handbag, but does not have a top that is covered so your pooch can pop their head out and watch the world go by.

Open carrier
Great for nosey
pooches.

Hands-free carrier – This enables you to carry your furbaby but also have your hands free. They generally go sling-style across your body, or you can get a front carrying bag that looks almost like a kangaroo pouch, which your little one sits in and faces forward. These are great if you need both hands.

Hands-free carrier
Just right for busy
furbaby mums.

Carrying your dog leaves you with one less arm for carting your own bits and pieces about. But that's the kind of sacrifice we owners of diva dogs make.

Not every dog needs a set of wheels but if, like me, you have a pack of pooches, you might find this the best way to get down the high street.

I was born to be wild!

TOP GEAR

Most strollers look very similar to baby buggies, and are often nicely coloured or patterned. You can get four- or three-wheel drive – just like the ones super-stylish new mums have.

The main difference between a human and a doggy stroller is the seating area. This is flat in a dog pram and has a mesh section plus lead safety attachments inside. Apart from that, they are pretty much the same.

COMFORT
ZONES

Your little diva naturally expects a 'rover-the-top' lifestyle, so give your sleeping beauty some super-special comfort spots for taking a well-earned catnap.

SWEET **DREAMS**

There's nothing a diva dog loves more than ultimate comfort and they all deserve somewhere super-cosy where they can have a nap or just chill out, away from the whirl of it all.

Your little diva will probably want to be in the same room as you, so one dog bed won't do. You'll need somewhere comfy for them in every room where they're likely to be spending time, unless you don't mind carrying their beds from place to place as they follow you around.

Lola has comfort spots in every room of the house. She even has a four-poster bed with silk cushions as well as a chaise longue. She's totally spoilt for choice, but she actually prefers a big duvet (the one on my bed!).

Before you take on a diva dog, you need to decide if you're happy for your little prince or princess to have an 'access all areas' pass or if you'd prefer to keep them off the bed or sofa. Whatever you decide, you'll need somewhere soft, safe and luxurious for your furbaby to sleep.

Cleanliness is next to dogliness, so make life easier for yourself by buying bedding that is machine-washable – even a diva dog doesn't expect their bedding to be dry-cleaned (although, I have to admit, Lola's four-poster has cushions that I would never trust to the spin cycle).

There are lots of amazing dog beds available these days in all sorts of colours, shapes and sizes. Plush faux fur is a particular favourite with dogs who want to kick back and unwind. With such an array of bed choices you can co-ordinate your dog's comfy places with the decor of your home or even have a bed custom-made.

Choose a bed that suits the way your little one likes to sleep. Some dogs prefer an open cushion so they can stretch and sprawl out while others like a circular bed where they can curl up in a tight little ball. If your furry one prefers to burrow under things, you can get snuggle sacks that are very similar to human sleeping bags. Just the thing for your sleeping snuggler.

Dog houses can be really cute and are great for dogs who will feel more secure in their enclosed mini-home. It's also nice to have a playpen so your pooch can entertain themselves in a place where you know they are safe.

Your lap is probably your little diva's favourite comfort zone, but some of these gorgeous beds come a very close second.

Dogs spend a total of about 12 hours a day sleeping and in between sleeps they like to doze, nap or just relax. No wonder, then, that they really appreciate some deluxe bedding where they can catch forty winks.

Your dog's bed is their very own space and one of the few things they don't share with you. It's the perfect place to take a favourite toy or hide a snack for later. After all, even the most sociable dog needs some alone time now and again.

DRESSED TO **IMPRESS**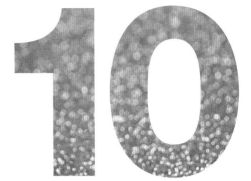

The diva dog likes to rise to the occasion and slip into something a little special from time to time. If your little show-off likes to step out in style, there's a great range of fabulous outfits to fill their wardrobe.

DO I LOOK
DOGGY-TASTIC IN THIS?

When I first got Lola, a doggy wardrobe overflowing with frilly dresses, patterned t-shirts and pink tutus couldn't have been further from my mind.

In the beginning, the whole doggy project had nothing whatsoever to do with fashion. Some people seem to think that small dogs are just fashion accessories, but that wasn't it at all as far as I was concerned.

But winter came along and my little Lola got very shivery. She would push her paws into the chilly ground and refuse to go for walks. It was obvious that she needed a coat to keep her warm and toasty. Lola's clothing habit began as a purely practical thing. However, the excitement of searching for totally cute products from all over the world for my new furry baby soon found me purchasing Lola's first outfit, which was a gorgeous cashmere sweater. After that, her wardrobe quickly expanded and nothing was too good for my little fashionista.

It's pretty obvious that Lola takes after me and loved being dressed up right from the start. Now she has hundreds of outfits and I have had a wardrobe custom-made to house all her precious ensembles. But not all dogs are so keen on being on the catwalk. My second dog, Lulu, for instance, never liked being dressed up. She is more of a tomboy

and favours the naturist way of life. I've always believed it's important to respect your pooch's personality; work with them – they'll tell you what they're happy wearing or, like Lulu, they may just prefer their birthday suit.

Of course, Lola doesn't wear clothes all the time, mostly she goes around stark naked just like any other dog, but it's so much fun to dress up for special occasions. Remember, if you want your diva to feel like a star, they'll need to be comfortable, so make sure you buy outfits that fit properly and suit your dog's breed and shape.

Lola is happy to wear coats and jumpers with arms and legs; she even puts her paws through the sleeves, almost as if she is dressing herself. It's super-cute, but not all dogs like the feeling of having their legs enclosed in this way. Certain breeds, dachshunds, for example, probably won't feel good with their little legs squeezed into trousers – they are normally too long for them, anyway. Chihuahuas can sometimes have quite full necks and need to wear clothes that allow room for movement. Pugs are known for having fairly deep chests so it's worth going for stretchy items that will be comfortable. Whatever look you go for, make sure you only buy clothes that are specially designed for doggies.

Classic dog coats are like a horse rug that fits over the dog's back, with fastenings over the chest and under the tummy. You might need a few different coats so your little love is properly protected in all weathers. Coats can be waterproof, warm, lined or unlined, and you can even get summer coats to keep them cool when it's hot. But why stop at a simple coat? These days, there are lots of other options for the fashion-conscious pup.

SPOILT FOR CHOICE

Some fashion items you might like to try:

♥ Hoodies – what diva doesn't look adorable in one of these?

♥ Vests and t-shirts – my favourites have funny slogans on them

♥ Dresses – make your pooch pretty as a picture

♥ Romper suits – they are little babies, after all

♥ Hair bows and clips – keep fringes out of eyes, plus they look cute

Mirror, mirror on the wall, who's the most stylish diva dog of all? It must be me!

Ludo wears a comfortable, low-key overcoat in a neutral pattern. Great for dogs who prefer outfits without enclosed legs.

Doggy clothes can be practical or fun, they can make your pooch look funny, cute or keep them warm. People sometimes find them amusing, but as long as your dog is comfortable they'll love the attention.

You can look but you can't touch

Baby Gracie is on trend with this animal print waterproof raincoat. It's lightweight, comfortable and protects in wet conditions.

Chloe looks fab in a patterned hoodie which is suitable for pooches who are happy wearing clothes. Can be worn in place of a coat on colder days.

Minnie is
pretty in a harness
dress – great for
pooches who want
to dress to impress.
The patterned
harness with an
attachable skirt
is guaranteed to
brighten dull days.

Betsey rocks
a waterproof all-in-one. Fantastic for snow and very wet or muddy conditions.

Baby Gracie
is chic in faux
fur-trimmed
waterproofs.
Perfect for looking
presentable
whatever the
weather.

Yoda does
summer wear with
a brightly coloured
t-shirt and matching
suncap. Just right to
keep the light from
your pooch's eyes
while still looking
über-trendy. Anyone
for ice cream?

Blue sports
a knitted jumper
– a must for dogs
with unusual body
frames. The stretch
in the material allows
for a comfortable
fit. Blue adores his
alpaca pullover.

FANCY **DRESS**

Fancy dress is very much for special occasions – poochie doesn't want to wear a fairy costume or bumblebee outfit all day any more than you would.

Fancy dress is fun – but use it sparingly. Your dog should always be supervised when in fancy dress and you need to be particularly careful with accessories such as fairy wings, which could cause a mishap.

If your little friend is timid or shy, don't put them in fancy dress. A dressed-up pooch will always attract attention, which could make a shy dog uncomfortable. If your diva is a natural show-off, there's nothing to hold you back – apart from your imagination and your budget.

DIVA DOG FANCY DRESS FAVOURITES
- Little devil
- Little stinker skunk
- Dogula vampire
- Angel
- Scary spider
- Bumblebee

LET'S GET THIS PARTY STARTED

11

Having a diva dog is such a joy it's only natural that you'll want to celebrate. Dogs are sociable creatures and they love to mix and mingle with other pooches and people. I feel a party coming on...

HOW TO HOST
A DOGGY CELEBRATION

Now, if, like me, you love parties almost as much as you love dogs, then why not organise a special occasion for your pooch and all their four-legged friends?

Personally, I love my parties to be OTT. Bring on the tiaras and the champagne frocks – what's a party without a touch of extravagance? I once organised a party for 350 furry guests – it was the social event of the doggy calendar. We had dancing ponies, a seven-foot-high dog-friendly chocolate fountain with pink – yes, pink – chocolate and gourmet bone-shaped dips. There was also a diva doggy fashion show that even had a swimwear collection. My Lola and her friends looked stunning strutting their stuff down the dogwalk. That first party was such a success that we've now made it an annual event, which gets bigger and bigger every time.

But if you prefer something more understated and intimate, your guests can have just as much fun at a quiet get-together with a few select friends. The key thing is that your party suits your dog's personality and your own personal tastes. The secret to a fabulous do is precision planning. So here are a few tips to help you organise the perfect party.

THINK OF A THEME
Who needs an excuse for a party? It's easy to find a reason to celebrate your favourite doggy. A puppy shower is a great way to introduce your young pooch to new people and pets. Birthdays, it goes without saying, are a time to show your dog some love. It's so much fun getting ready for birthdays – after all, we celebrate our own birthdays, don't we?

Then, of course, there is Christmas, Easter and Halloween. If you want something more personal, why not choose your own theme? Think of the great costumes you could get for a Barbie-themed party, a fairy-tale prince and princess party… or you could choose a favourite film for inspiration, like *Legally Blonde* or *Beverly Hills Chihuahua* – that's got to be one of my all-time greats. There are no hard-and-fast rules with parties; just make them as exciting or as silly as you want.

Doggy parties are great fun, but they can also be an opportunity to do good for dogs who are less fortunate than our own loved-up pooches. With our huge doggy parties we always try to raise awareness and money for charity. If you're organising a party for charity, don't be afraid to ask for help. You'll be surprised how many people will be ready to chip in if they think it's for a good cause.

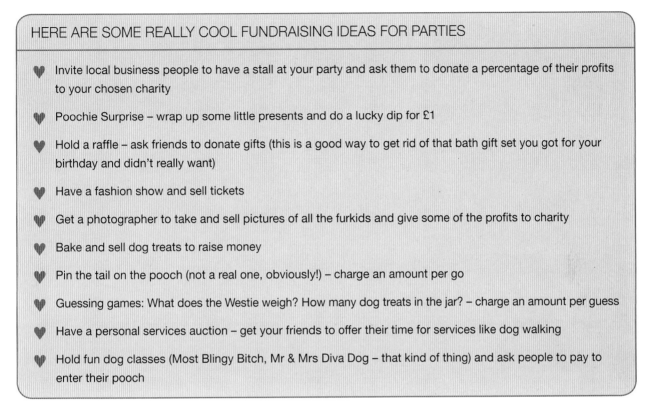

HERE ARE SOME REALLY COOL FUNDRAISING IDEAS FOR PARTIES

💜 Invite local business people to have a stall at your party and ask them to donate a percentage of their profits to your chosen charity

💜 Poochie Surprise – wrap up some little presents and do a lucky dip for £1

💜 Hold a raffle – ask friends to donate gifts (this is a good way to get rid of that bath gift set you got for your birthday and didn't really want)

💜 Have a fashion show and sell tickets

💜 Get a photographer to take and sell pictures of all the furkids and give some of the profits to charity

💜 Bake and sell dog treats to raise money

💜 Pin the tail on the pooch (not a real one, obviously!) – charge an amount per go

💜 Guessing games: What does the Westie weigh? How many dog treats in the jar? – charge an amount per guess

💜 Have a personal services auction – get your friends to offer their time for services like dog walking

💜 Hold fun dog classes (Most Blingy Bitch, Mr & Mrs Diva Dog – that kind of thing) and ask people to pay to enter their pooch

CHOOSE A VENUE

The most obvious place to hold your pooch party is at your own home. If this is the case, you have to make sure you have a garden secure enough to prevent even the tiniest dog from escaping. If you're planning on staying outside, do you have a plan B if it starts raining? If you're going to invite your guests into the house, remember that even the best-dressed pooches may have a lapse in manners – don't invite lots of dogs into your home if you can't cope with a pee incident or a little mayhem. Even princes and princesses can sometimes get a little overexcited. They can also get very vocal, so think carefully about who and how many guests you invite.

If you plan to hire a venue, make sure it's truly dog-friendly. I've come across this problem a few times myself and my advice is to ask the venue the following questions:

• Are dogs allowed into all areas of the venue?
• Are there poop bins or facilities to dispose of waste?
• Are there facilities to get water for your guests?
• If you require power, is this available?
• Can you bring dog food and treats into the venue? (Some venues will not allow it.)
• Do they have parking facilities for your guests?
• Can you get access early enough to have time to set everything up?

Every party is different and you may need to ask if they have a licence for music or lighting for the dogwalk. Whatever you do, try to think of every possible question relating to your party.

CANINE **CATERING**

A good party host always provides refreshments for their guests, but extra-special care is needed when those guests have eyes bigger than their stomachs.

Dogs can be greedy and will eat whatever they can find, so don't put food where they can help themselves – let their human friends decide what and how much they should eat.

If you do provide doggy snacks, make sure they are healthy. Sugary snacks are never a good idea and remember – never give chocolate to a dog unless it's specifically made for dogs. No party host wants their guests to be sick or, worse still, seriously ill because of bad catering.

Unlike some of their owners, dogs are lucky enough to be able to enjoy themselves without alcohol, but they still need a drink so don't forget to provide plenty of doggy water bowls.

You can also buy specially made birthday cakes, carob-topped doggy lollipops, popcorn for dogs and dog-friendly cookies. You could even bake your own yummy treats, like Lola's favourite special occasion doggy recipe – liver love hearts.

LOLA'S LIVER LOVE HEARTS

INGREDIENTS
2 cups wholewheat flour
⅓ cup butter, melted
1 egg, beaten
6 tablespoons water
¼ cup finely chopped liver

METHOD
1. Preheat the oven to 180°C/350°F/gas mark 4 and grease a baking sheet.
2. Combine the flour, butter, egg and water and mix together well (a mixer comes in handy here). Add the chopped liver.
3. Place the mixture on to a floured surface, making it about 1 in (2.5 cm) thick. Use a heart-shaped cookie cutter to cut out some liver hearts.
4. Transfer the liver hearts to the baking sheet and bake for 20–25 minutes until golden brown.
5. Leave the hearts to cool down before serving to your little pampered pooch.

FUN AND **GAMES**

Some of the things that humans find very entertaining are actually quite frightening to dogs. Balloons, party poppers, sparklers and fireworks are not a dog's idea of a good time.

A good host doesn't spook the guests, so use your imagination to come up with activities that dogs will enjoy. Dogs love playing and anything you can do to encourage your human guests to interact with their furkids will go down really well. Here are some suggestions:

Pass the pawcel – Wrap up a treat and pass it around in a circle. When the music stops, the owner unwraps the next layer of paper.

Play fetch – Most dogs really enjoy this.

Hide and seek – Hide a really tasty treat and let the dogs have fun seeking it out. This is great around Easter, when they can do a hunt for a bone-shaped dog biscuit rather than an egg.

Best trick competition – Can your dog sit, roll over, speak or maybe just look super-duper cute?

THE GUEST LIST

No matter how much you like a particular dog (or the dog's human friend) only invite genuine party animals to your do. Don't invite dogs who are shy or nervous – some dogs just don't enjoy socialising. Leave very boisterous dogs off your guest list, too.

Nobody likes an overbearing guest, and you want all the pooches at your party to feel at ease.

Remember, a diva dog loves going to parties and will always want to look their best – after all, that's what divas do.

INDEX

ACKNOWLEDGEMENTS

I'd like to thank my original diva dog, Lola, my inspiration! Without my bundle of fluff I can only assume I'd still be working in the City doing a job I hate, clock-watching and living for the weekend. Lola changed my life. I was given a blessing in the form of a Yorkshire terrier and for that I will be forever grateful.

To my other three amazing, adorable furbabies, Lulu, Lolly and my boy Larry. Every day you make me smile, you complete my life. THANK YOU.

A special thank you to my mummy diva, Janet Sapiano, without whose ambition, courage and fighting spirit I may have been a completely different person. Her support, hard work and belief in me have made this possible. You are the best mummy diva EVER!

To my amazing aunt, Julie Grice, who has helped more than anyone can imagine. You have always been there.

Thank you to my nan and grand – the whirlwind has been tamed…finally.

My partner Daniel Hill – I love you and thank you. If it was easy, everyone would do it.

A special thank you to:
Each and every diva-ette – without your support and diva love none of this would be possible. You're the best!

All of Lola's friends, especially Baby Gracie, Bella, Betsey, Betty, Billy, Blue, Bow, Chloe, Daisy, Ellie, Gremlin, Ludo, Minnie, Molly, Roley, Ruby Roo, Rudi, Tia Maria and Yoda.

Justine Hankins, Stuart Cooper, Francine Lawrence, Nigel Wright and Lorraine Jerram.

Craig Lees, my BFF – no matter how much time passes it always seems like only yesterday.
Jane Gallant Hall – you're fab, always there when I need you, even with tight deadlines.
Louise Birch – keep up the hard work girl… Final push!
Helen Latimer of Latimer Couture (www.latimercouture.com) for making me beautiful every day.
Hair stylists Silhouette du Barry (www.sdbhair.co.uk).
My amazing stylist Donna Louise (www.donnalouisestyle.co.uk).
Anya's Closet (www.anyascloset.com) and my amazing evening dress stylist, Nadia, and girls.
Penny at Pia Michi (www.piamichi.com).
Models of Diversity (www.modelsofdiversity.org).
Laura at Love Lemonade (www.lovelemonade.com).